THE CHRISTIAN FAITH AND YOUTH TODAY

PROCEEDINGS OF

THE CONFERENCE ON RELIGION IN EDUCATION

UNDER THE AUSPICES OF

THE COUNCIL FOR RELIGION IN INDEPENDENT SCHOOLS

HELD AT

Atlantic City, October, 1956

THE
CHRISTIAN FAITH
AND
YOUTH TODAY

Edited By

MALCOLM STRACHAN and ALVORD M. BEARDSLEE

GREENWICH CONNECTICUT

19   57

PREFACE

From the afternoon of October 18th, 1956, until noon on October 20th, three hundred and fifty-one persons from one hundred and sixty-two schools from Maine to Florida and from New York to California, met at the Hotel Dennis in Atlantic City to study and discuss the question of how the insights of psychology and religion can contribute to our understanding of youth. This was in one respect an historic occasion, for it was the first conference held in the name of the Council for Religion in Independent Schools. In its earlier life as the National Preparatory School Committee of the Y.M.C.A., four conferences had been held—in 1932, 1938, 1946, and 1950. Though the one held in October 1956, and recorded in this volume, follows in the general tradition of those earlier conferences, it was the first to be called by the Council under its new name and in complete independence of the Y.M.C.A.

A committee, headed by E. Lawrence Springer, headmaster of The Pingry School, worked on this conference for well over a year. It was no easy task to plan a program designed to meet religious needs, offer strength for academic standards of courses in religion, and enlarge the spiritual vision of teachers from as wide a variety of schools as were to be represented at this gathering. Yet such aims in fact epitomize the purpose of all the Council's work, of which this three-day conference was a concentrated expression. To it were drawn representatives from church and non- church schools— boarding, day, girls', boys', co-educational, military—mostly secondary but some primary schools. The participants were as diverse as the schools. Seated side by side were women garbed in the habit of their orders, laymen and women who either administer their schools or teach in classes or act as counseling specialists, and, of course, many clergymen. Almost every variety of Christian faith, outside Roman Catholicism, was represented among those who responded to *The Call*.

In the light of such diversity of background and conviction it should be said that neither the contents of this book nor the unpublished records of discussion groups represents a unanimously agreed upon position on the part of members of the Conference. This book should rather be looked upon as something of a reflection of the climate of religious education in the independent school today.

A searching interest in the subject of the conference was evident from the start, and the number of people present who had attended the Council's Yale Institute or Faculty Colloquia indicated that much of the interest was informed. The quality of the questions and discussions confirmed these early indications. High though the intellectual tone of the gathering was, this would not alone have made for its strength. Beneath all the talk and work, there was an infectious warmth and friendliness that made the conference more like a family gathering. The three principal speakers themselves noted this and responded wholeheartedly, mingling freely and informally with the members and entering into every side of their interests.

The meeting was an inspiring and strengthening one, and had its moments of rapt attention. When Dr. Cleland closed the conference with a benediction, one sensed that it had been far more than a routine occasion. It had been an exciting exploration into the Christian undergirding and spiritual implications of all our work as schoolmasters.

—THE EDITORS

CONTENTS

THE OPENING
OF THE CONFERENCE

The Address of Welcome

BY E. LAURENCE SPRINGER

HEADMASTER OF THE PINGRY SCHOOL AND CONFERENCE CHAIRMAN

On behalf of the sponsoring committee of the Council for Religion in Independent Schools, I welcome you to this Conference on *Religion in Education*. Some three hundred and seventy of us are here from more than one hundred and sixty different schools. We have come here from many parts of the country, and we have come with sincere intent and deep concern, seeking insights from our religion and from psychology, so that we may be of greater service to the young people in our schools.

Others of you have come here seeking assistance in the techniques of teaching. We have made provisions for you, too. For whatever the reason you have come, you are indeed welcome. We are delighted to see you here.

I should like to open our conference formally by reading THE CALL.

The Call

'To be a schoolmaster', wrote Erasmus long years ago, 'is next to being a king. Do you count it a mean employment to imbue the minds of your fellow citizens in their earnest years with the best literature and with the love of Christ, and to return them to their country honest and virtuous men?'

The young people of our schools face a confused world. Insensitivity to their personal needs, temptations to waste their talents, and loud invitations to moral laxity confront them at every turn. The guidance which religion and psychology offer is often misunderstood and misapplied. Christianity, which adolescents frequently consider to be primarily a moral code, seems to present to their impatient eyes only outdated rules and unreal restrictions. Religion may appear too demanding on the one hand, and unrelated to present problems on the other.

In the light of this, how do we 'return them to their country honest and virtuous men'? Most certainly we cannot lead others where we ourselves have not been. We cannot produce in others what we ourselves have not achieved, nor even understand.

To study and discuss these questions, we invite Headmistresses and Headmasters and their colleagues to the 1956 Conference on Religion in Education to be held in Atlantic City on October 18-20. Here we shall have unhurried opportunity to quicken within ourselves a spiritual awareness that we hope may come to be reflected in the lives of the young people whom we guide; to consider the relationship of Christianity and the scientific insights of our minds and emotions to the immediate problems of the students in our schools; and to seek methods of leading our pupils to the establishment of worthy values.

We issue this Call in the urgent hope that you will join with us as together we seek these goals.

Let us rise for the invocation.

The Invocation

Almighty and merciful heavenly Father, who art the source of love and truth, be with us we pray, in this conference. Through inspired men and women of the past and of the present, we have gained some insights of thy will and of thy plan and purpose for us. Especially through thy Son, Jesus Christ, we have an example of the true meaning of love and of the attitudes we as teachers should assume toward those entrusted to our care. Through men of science, we have learned much concerning human nature and the causes of mental illness and health. May these insights be made clearer to us as we gather here to think and discuss together the problems of youth. Forgive our transgressions against our young people and our neglect of their deepest needs. Fill our hearts with a desire to minister to them in the spirit in which Jesus ministered to those who were sick in body, in mind, in soul. And above all we pray that thy Holy Spirit may descend on us, touching our hearts and souls, and quickening our spiritual understanding, to the end that we may better serve the youth of our schools, and thus better serve thee. We ask these things in the name of Jesus Christ our Lord. *Amen.*

The theme of our conference—the insights of religion and psychology—I think you will agree, is a reflection of the times in which we live. Thirty-five years ago a conference with a theme of this sort would have been impossible. Religion and science had not yet finished their great struggle. Watson, in psychology, was in the ascendancy with his theories of behaviorism, and no rapport between psychology and religion would have been possible.

Our times have been referred to by various names, such as the Atomic Age, or the Age of Chaos, or the Age of Frustration, or the Age of Anxiety. By whatever name we wish to call the one in which we live, we know that mankind desperately needs saving. He needs certainly the insights of religion and psychology.

I need not point out to this group the increased religious interest on the campuses of our colleges and schools. Nor need I emphasize to you the importance of psychology in education, in personnel work, in guidance and in pastoral work; nor need I emphasize the popular demand for self-help books, which indicates the need people feel for greater sources of power and strength than they find within themselves.

If mankind in general, in the middle of the twentieth century, needs the help of religion and psychology, how particularly do we teachers need this help, not only for ourselves but for the guidance of those who are entrusted to our

3

care? Our boys and girls have their problems. They have their frustrations and their deep needs, and they look to us for guidance.

The planning committee of this conference was convinced that our theme was timely and needed. Your committee has been working and planning for a year and a half. Having chosen the theme, we then tried to find speakers equal to the challenge. Our specifications were high, and truly it was no small task to find men who are both dedicated Christians, capable of giving us the insights of religion, and also fully aware of the implications and importance of psychology. We wanted men who were not living in ivory towers, however learned they might be, but we wanted men who are in close contact with youth, who understood their needs and their problems. Our speakers are all qualified by their education and experience to show us how the insights of psychology and religion can help us solve the problems of youth. Each of these three men will address us on one aspect of the theme, and each of these men will lead us in a service of worship. Our speaker this evening will discuss the insights of religion; our speaker tomorrow morning will consider the insights of psychology; and on Saturday morning our third speaker will synthesize the talks and the theme of the conference as it has developed. The conference program offers plenty of opportunity for discussion. We plan that through the discussion groups you may pursue the topics which the three speakers have presented.

JAMES T. CLELAND:

A PRACTICAL CHRISTIANITY

THE REVEREND JAMES T. CLELAND was born in Glasgow, Scotland in 1903. He was educated at Glasgow University and later on at Union Theological Seminary in New York City. It was at Union that he received the degree of Master of Sacred Theology. Davison College has awarded him an honorary doctorate in Divinity. He has taught at Glasgow and at Amherst. In 1938 he was ordained to the ministry of the Presbyterian Church. Since 1945 he has been Professor of Preaching and Preacher to the University at Duke. He is the author of many articles in various publications, and is among those who have contributed expositions to the Interpreter's Bible.

A
PRACTICAL
CHRISTIANITY

You have heard the Call; it is a good statement. It reveals the alert awareness of sensitive Christian men and women both to the culture in which our schools are set and to the needs of their clientele: to imbue the minds of our students with the best literature and with the love of Christ, and to return them to their country honest and virtuous.

Now, let me narrow the Call to my particular task by referring to the assignment given me for this occasion. I have been asked to present Christianity today, not primarily from a theological viewpoint or in theological terms (an impossible task) but in practical working terms that would be understandable to heads of schools; and I am asked to do this in non-denominational terms. This, as you may guess, is quite an assignment. One would need the intellectual prowess of an Erasmus, plus the tongues of men and angels, to do the job. Even then, you and I would be required to possess charity and still more charity, or else the outcome would be sounding brass or, worse, a tinkling cymbal.

I

Let me try to assess the human situation in which our discussion has to be set, and also offer two caveats. You represent, in the main, three different types of school, though there is an inevitable overlapping in the categories. You yourselves cannot always decide in which category your particular school falls. Moreover, your student body is a heterogeneous, non-conforming, melee of youth when viewed from any one of the standpoints.

1. *The Liberal Arts School.* This is the kind of school which draws on Protestants, Jews, Roman Catholics, and vague agnostics, and prepares them for entry to college. It recognizes that Christianity has been a formative influence in the culture of the Western world and, as such, has a rightful place in any Liberal Arts program. Therefore, such schools are willing to sponsor courses in religion, where the Bible is read as living literature. They may even add to this a daily chapel period (though not a Sunday service) which validly places a religious imprimatur on the more sensitive ethical mores of the community.

2. *The More Consciously Christian School.* This second type of school differs from the first in that it is aware of the influence of Christianity on the heart and will, as well as on the mind. It offers classes in religion, outside of the English Department. It reckons with the critical approach to the Bible. It is interested in Christian ethics in the modern world. In its chapel, and especially, in the Sunday service, sermonettes are offered, often by so-called distinguished ministers, to inspire religious living on a spiritually elevated plane.

3. *The Committed Christian School.* This is the school which is consciously Protestant and denominational. The Holy Communion is regularly celebrated, or periods of Quaker silence are rigorously observed. A chapel building is set apart for services of worship, which are liturgically and ceremonially dignified. Courses are offered on biblical theology and on the history of Christian ideas. It knows a prayer book and *The Interpreter's Bible.* It prepares young people to become members of one branch of the Church.

Perhaps, that brief sketch of your human situation will

give you some idea of my problem in addressing all of you, at one and the same time, on the Christian faith.

Let us turn now to the two caveats.

First of all, the older I grow, the more convinced I become that Christianity is a religion of maturity. Some divinity students at Duke University came to me once and asked what one fact about Jesus they should never forget. I suggested that it was that Jesus kept his mouth shut until he was thirty. (I also suggested that they go and do likewise.) At that point I probably clash with Professor Hans Hofmann. I hope he can persuade me otherwise, but there does seem to me to be a problem here which I cannot solve but which I wish to recognize with regard to Christianity and youth.

In the second place, Christianity is in conflict with the prevailing, national world-view in America. That may seem an absurd statement in the light of the Christian revival in our midst. Yet, what we are observing is an adulterated Christianity. It is almost the worship of Baal with a Yahweh ritual. It does tinge self-interest with benevolence. But real Christianity seems to be contrary, for our thinking youngsters, to the normal American outlook. It may be suitable for clergymen, and Sundays, and weddings, and funerals, but it is not of major importance for ordinary living.

With that glimpse at the human situation and the awareness of the two caveats, let us, as they say in Scotland, get tore into the subject assigned.

II

We are so used, by an understandable custom, to dividing the Bible into the Old Testament and the New Testament, into the Jewish religion and the Christian religion, into B.C. and A.D., that we sometimes miss the essential fact of the whole Bible. The Bible, taken as a whole, is constantly conscious that the problem of the religious norm centers in a fundamental conflict between two ideas: the idea of Faith and the idea of Law. What do we mean by each of these ideas? 'Faith' is a short hand way of saying that the focus of religious experience lies in the willing acceptance by man of the fact that God wishes, wills, and seeks constantly to bring man into right relations with himself. Man receives the gracious love of God. Religion is the reception of that good will and our glad response to it. 'Law' is a short hand way of saying that the center of religious experience lies in the earnest activity of man to obey the detailed requirements of God and, thus, to make himself worthy to be accepted by God. Man is on the active end of persuading God to receive him because of his good works. Religion consists in good works done for this purpose. The dichotomy is not an absolute one. But, for purposes of examination, let us look at it thus, even though some of you rightly complain that there is an element of caricature in this presentation. Others of you are willing to accept these two ideas as presented, provided that Law is retained as the key word of the Old Testament religion and Faith as the key word of New Testament religion. But the point I am seeking to make now is that this is not so. Faith and Law are found side by side in both the Old Testament and the New Testament. The Old Testament and the New Testament are confronted with the same problem: the conflict of the religion of Faith and the religion of Law. The division should not be a vertical one *between* the Testaments, but a horizontal one *within* each Testament.

Let me illustrate this proposition from four sections of the Bible.

We are all aware of the antagonism between the legalist and the prophet. The early Old Testament legal systems emphasized the concept of sacrifice: the sin offering, the first fruits, the cereal offering, and the like. It was an elaborate cultic system, carried out with devotion and with enthusiasm. Chapter after chapter of Deuteronomy and Leviticus shows the compelling importance of sacrifice in the minds and hearts of the Jewish people. Yet, listen to the prophet speak about it. Here are some verses from Amos:

'I hate, I despise your feasts,
and I take no delight in your solemn assemblies.
Even though you offer me your
burnt offerings and cereal offerings,
I will not accept them,
and the peace offerings of your fatted beasts
I will not look upon.
Take away from me the noise of your songs;
to the melody of your harps I will not listen.
But let justice roll down like waters,
and righteousness like an ever-flowing stream.'

Listen to Micah:

'With what shall I come before the Lord,
and bow myself before God on high?
Shall I come before him with burnt offerings,
with calves a year old?
Will the Lord be pleased with thousands of rams,
with ten thousands of rivers of oil?
Shall I give my first-born for my transgression,
the fruit of my body for the sin of my soul?
He has showed you, O man, what is good;
and what does the Lord require of you
but to do justice, and to love kindness,
and to walk humbly with your God?'

Now, on what do such men dare to base their criticism of religion as Law? It is rooted in their estimate of the character of God. He is a God who requires of man only justice and mercy, in addition to adoration. Why? Because he wishes man to be like him, and he is just and merciful. The outcome of that struggle was what you might have guessed.

There was a compromise. The late prophets, such as Ezekiel and Malachi, combine in their point of view a combination of their appreciation of the character of God and an elaborate system of priestly offerings.

One sees a similar compromise in the Psalms. The book of Psalms is the hymn book of the Second Temple and, side by side, are poems which praise the Law and poems which are grounded in Faith, in the undemanding mercy of God. The 1st Psalm loves the Law. Listen to it:

'Blessed is the man
　who walks not in the counsel of the wicked,
　nor stands in the way of sinners,
　　nor sits in the seat of scoffers;
　but his delight is in the law of the Lord,
　and on his law he meditates day and night.'

The longest chapter in the Bible, one hundred and seventy-six verses, makes up the 119th Psalm and it, too, is legal from stem to stern. Here is how it begins:

'Blessed are those whose way is blameless,
　who walk in the law of the Lord!
Blessed are those who keep his testimonies,
　who seek him with their whole heart.'

Its constant refrain is:

'Teach me, oh Lord, the way of they statutes,
　and I will keep it to the end.'

But there is another mood in the Psalms, a mood that is shot through with what we have called Faith. Listen to the opening of the 40th Psalm:

'I waited patiently for the Lord;
　he inclined to me and heard my cry.
He drew me up from the desolate pit,
　out of the miry bog, and set my feet upon a rock,
　making my steps secure.
He put a new song in my mouth,
　a song of praise to our God.'

Add to these verses Psalm 23, The Shepherd Psalm, and you appreciate the other strain in Faith: dependence on the loving mercy of God.

Turn now to the New Testament. The Pharisees and their followers laid great stress on the keeping of the Sabbath; on proper methods of washing before a meal; on the avoidance of contact with 'sinners.' Jesus' complaint was not that they were utterly wrong, but that they were missing the central truth in religion. They were so obsessed with the minutiae of the Law that they forgot what God was like and what he really wanted. That is why Jesus spoke that terrible 23rd Chapter of Matthew. Here are two verses from it: 'Woe to you, scribes and Pharisees, hypocrites! for you tithe mint and dill and cummin, and have neglected the weightier matters of the law, justice, and mercy, and faith; these you ought to have done, without neglecting the others. You blind guides, straining out a gnat, and swallowing a camel!' How he must have loved that straining out a gnat (in Palestine of all places!) and then swallowing a camel. Can you see it go down, hump and all? If you want to know what God is really like, then listen to verse 37 of the same chapter: 'O Jerusalem, Jerusalem, that killeth the prophets, and stoneth them that are sent unto her! How often would I have gathered thy children together, even as a hen gathereth her chickens under her wings, and ye would not!' Jesus acts toward man as he believes God does, and God is a God who gathers together the outcasts. Why? Because that is his nature; he cannot help it.

Let us take a fourth and last example. There was a group of men in the early Church who came to be known as the Judaizers. They insisted that before a person could become a Christian, he must become a Jew. He must keep the Law. In order to enter the Church, one must pass through the synagogue. In the Epistle to the Galatians, Paul dynamited that idea and blew it to smithereens. A man is not saved by keeping the Law; a man is saved by Faith—a man is saved by his confidence that God means well by him. Here are three verses from the 5th chapter of that plea for Christian freedom:

'For freedom Christ has set us free;
stand fast therefore, and do not submit again
to a yoke of slavery.

Now I, Paul, say to you that if you receive
circumcision, Christ will be of no advantage to you.'

Paul is a preacher, and on that point he is overemphatic as most preachers are. But he is making the point that circumcision does not count. What does count? Faith! Faith working through love. 'For in Christ Jesus neither circumcision nor uncircumcision is of any avail, but faith working through love.'

Do you see now what I mean when I say that the proper division of the Bible is not a vertical one *between* the Old Testament and the New, but a horizontal one *within* each Testament?

The Gospel, that is, the good news about God and his dealings with men, is in both the Old Testament and the New. After all, God is the same, yesterday, today, and forever. You do not expect him to change his attitude to man. In case you think this is just a Clelandian heresy, listen to No. VII of The Articles of Religion as found in the Book of Common Prayer: 'The Old Testament is not contrary to the New, for both in the Old and New Testament everlasting life is offered to Mankind by Christ, who is the only Mediator between God and Man, being both God and Man.' Before you comment that it is hardly valid evidence for a Presbyterian to quote an Episcopalian document, let me tell you that that sentence, repeated word for word, is Article VI of the Articles of Religion as published in *Doctrines and Discipline of the Methodist Church.*

III

A number of years ago some students and a professor in the Duke Divinity School, after much debate and with numerous emendations, wrote a creed. Let me quote it to you: 'God, the Creator and Sustainer of life, has so purposed in his love that man be in right relations with him, that of his own free will he overcomes the power and erases the guilt of sin which separates man from God. This was always his effective purpose, but it was uniquely manifested and dramatized in the birth, life, death, and resurrection of Jesus. He is acknowledged as the Son of God because he supremely reveals the will and nature of God. This redeeming activity of God is perpetuated by the working of the Holy Spirit. Those who believe this are bound in an eternal fellowship whose daily life on earth is marked by faith, love, and hope. Those who refuse to believe this are under the judgment of God's love, here and hereafter.'

That attempt to state the Word of God is not perfect. We have enough of a sense of humor, if not of humility, to refuse to believe that creation has been groaning and travailing for hundreds of years to produce a professor and a class which would say the definitive word on the Word of God. But we believe we are not entirely wrong.

You may wish to add to that creed, saying more about Jesus Christ and about his Cross. But they will be additions rather than emendations of the basic biblical truth that, from Genesis to Revelation, God goes out in love to man. Despite man's misunderstanding of God's desire, despite his refusal of God's offer of friendship, despite his seeking the meaning of life in himself, God keeps coming back with yet another offer of good understanding. God does not do this because man deserves it or works for it, but because that is the kind of God he is—a God of love, of good will to man. That

activity of God, seen in so many events in the pages of the
Old and New Testaments, is what is meant by *salvation* and
justification and *adoption* and *redemption* and the like.
That is the 'Good News' of the Bible from beginning to end.
It is the Gospel found in Exodus as in Matthew, preached
by Second Isaiah and by St. Paul, broadcast by the Book of
the Law in 621 B.C. and incarnated in Jesus at the beginning
of the Christian Era. The God, who is the same yesterday,
today and forever, never had any other purpose for man
from the creation until now. Therefore, thanks be to God
for his unspeakable gift, which he was always giving and
which was uniquely revealed in Jesus Christ, our Lord. The
Incarnation is but the biblical climax of a repeated revelation. It is the norm of the religion of Faith, because it sums
up in itself the purpose of God as understood throughout
the Bible.

You say to me, 'Sir, isn't this focusing on Faith an easier
religion than one focused on Law?' This may seem so at
first, but it is not so later for the average person. It is easier
to keep the Law than to love God like a son, because it is
easier for us to observe legal requirements than to live God's
life after him. A law is static; the life of a son is dynamic,
ever widening, ever deepening. Listen to this poem written
by a girl who graduated with a B.D. degree last year at Union
Theological Seminary. It is called, 'The Prayer of a Near
Christian.' It is a fine piece of work theologically and
poetically.

> 'I do not want to serve Thee, Lord, but if I must,
> Please let it be some less consuming way.
> Why it is that a God must choose to tie
> His people to Him with the strongest means
> He has created? If I am Thy child,
> Remove from me this burden of Thy love
> And let me serve Thee in a lesser way.

Oh, now I understand how Israel could choose
To be Thy servant rather than Thy son!
I am too cowardly to be Thy child—
Let me, like Israel, serve Thee under Law
And find Thy love therein. This is too close
For me to stand; Thou knowest me too well,
And I can see myself for what I am
Reflected with a damning clarity
Against the measure of Thy first-born Son.
Release me, Lord, and let me worship Thee
A little farther off, and keep my pride.'

There's the rub. The religion of Law lets us keep our pride—the ultimate sin. The religion of Faith demands our initial humility and offers ultimate blessedness.

Let me try to illustrate this Faith in picture form. Think of two sons, twin sons, living at home and working on their father's farm. They do the same chores every day; each completes the same amount of work as the other. When the result of their respective work is measured, it comes out even. Yet, there is a difference between them, personally. The difference is seen in their names. One is called Law; the other, Faith. Wherein lies the difference? It is twofold. First, it is in motivation. Law does his work so that, at the end of the day, he may hear the words: 'Well done, good and faithful servant.' Faith does his work because he already knows he is the beloved son of his father. You can point the difference in another way: in the look on their faces. Law shows the marks of tension, in his worried striving to be considered worthy. Faith has no lines of strain because he has already received the highest title a man can have— 'Son,' 'Son of the Father.' The man who lives by Faith lives with no anxiety at the heart of his being, however much he may wrestle with problems of technique, as he seeks to implement and apply his Faith. He knows that the full Christian life is an 'impossible possibility' so long as man is on earth, cribbed, cabined, and confined in the flesh, and so long as he has a double allegiance to church and state. Even so, his experience of God is a joyous fact, and his expression of it is to live the life of a son, to the best of his ability, here on earth.

Now, a religion centered on Faith will do something to ourselves and to our techniques as we work with prep school boys and girls. As children of God, we shall treat them as potential children of God. More than that, when they ask us, we shall be able to give reasons for our conduct, because our conduct is based upon our interpretation of the character and the will of God as revealed in Holy Scripture and constantly revealed in Jesus Christ.

Let me now touch tentatively on the 'why' of Christianity. Why is it important for our prep schools to know the 'why'?

First, it is important culturally. We had better know the Jewish Christian strain in our heritage. No one is educated who is not at home in the Bible and does not know its development in historical-ecclesiastical theology. The Christian world-view has had an influence on literature, painting, architecture, law, and ethics. Colleges and universities, with their growing departments of religion, are more and more conscious of this. It is the arduous privilege of the prep schools to lay the groundwork.

Secondly, it is important ideologically. The average person wants and needs a self-committal to the more-than-self. The question constantly troubling him is which more-than-self will he commit himself to, and what happens when these seemingly ultimate goods are in conflict? A real study of comparative religion for American youth would not deal with Mohammedanism, Hinduism, and Buddhism, but it would deal with Capitalism, Nationalism, Socialism, and Communism. Of course, there has been invalid intermarriage among these ideas with a resultant crop of illegitimate offspring. It is our task to explain with accuracy and under-stand, the Jewish-Christian more-than-self, its promises and its demands.

Thirdly, it is important psychologically. This is Dr. Hof-mann's task, but let me comment briefly on it. The desire for commitment to the more-than-self is often located in the longing for security. We want to be safely at home even in the world, or perhaps better, even on earth. Security, in turn, has a double emphasis: individually and community-wise. The young person wishes to be a person in his own right, but it is in some sort of community that he best finds himself. The most common expression of this in a boy's school is symbolized in the solidarity evoked by athletic con-tests in which the individual can 'let himself go' for the school. What Christianity says about the individual *within* community does grant this security.

Culturally, ideologically and psychologically, there is an arresting 'why' for Christianity and the Christian life in our day in our job.

Granted the validity, (and that is a tremendous thing to grant), of the 'what' and 'why', let us turn to the 'how' of Christianity. How do we explicate and implement the Christian faith within the school?

First, the classroom. Because God is truth and because he is revealed historically in a body of content—the Bible, the creeds, the hymns, the prayers, the 'saints'—there is need for the expert, the teacher trained in religious data, to give instruction in the field. The scholarly objectivity of such a teacher means that he does not abuse or misuse the faith in any realm. There is a place for the lecture—on the Bible, on the creeds, on church history, and on the 'saints.' Doctrinal courses should be offered where possible. Care should always be taken that religious study is not merely literary in character, and not the private preserve of the English depart-ment. The lectures should be supplemented by discussion.

I know many of us do not like the discussion method. Some of us are not any good at it, that is why we do not like it. Others of us cannot believe that if you pool enough ignorance, truth will emerge. Discussion leading requires an unique type of training. But a good lecturer can be a leader of a discussion group, if he cultivates patience, sympathy, and a capacity for keeping his own mouth shut for over long periods. It is possible. It is not probable; but it is possible.

Second, the chapel. Since God is holy, it is essential that regular periods be set apart for our worship of him in the schools, that is, in those schools which are not merely in the Liberal Arts tradition. Corporate worship can be the expression of the entire school, both students and masters, in spiritual community. Some of you will stress a disciplined ceremony; others of you emphasize intellectual dignity throughout the service; yet others prefer the family-worship type of service. But whichever is chosen, let there be explanation of the 'why' and 'what' of the particular form of service you use. In addition, help should be given the student in the cultivation and expression of his own private individual appreciation of the holiness of God. Did you ever explain to your pupils the whole gamut of prayer: adoration, confession, thanksgiving, intercession, supplication, and dedication? There are numerous good books of school prayers which can be placed in their hands. We must help them to be helped with commentaries and the like, to make their devotional reading intelligible.

Then, in the third place, service. Because God is love and because he exposes his followers to love, opportunity should be given for the expression of good will to others. Lasting inspiration follows sound instruction and young people need guidance. How do you use your money? How much do you have? What do you do with it? Where did it come from? How do you use your time? How do your use your talents? How should you use them? It is still true that he who does the will of God begins to understand the doctrines. Service and worship and study are a trinity in Faith.

IV

It is very necessary for us to recognize that the Incarnation is not an event which happened but once, but a perennial occurrence. The concept of the Holy Spirit and the experience of the pioneers of the Faith of all ages, point to the fact that the Word, to be understood, must become flesh in every generation. At this point, the three types of schools mentioned in the introduction can be pulled together. In any school, in every subject, a Christian can show himself a Christian by the way he teaches anything, by the way he behaves anywhere. Sincerity is essential; so is sympathy, which goes away beyond the Renaissance virtue of tolerance. A Christian teacher experiences all the longings of his students. He laughs with those who laugh and weeps with those who weep. He may weep for those who laugh, but he would not often laugh at those who weep—except in private. Perhaps in this way, best of all, he prepares his pupils for the demands which life constantly makes, and watches them leave the school 'honest and virtuous' which was what Erasmus desired.

SERVICE OF WORSHIP

Dr. Mollegen

It is not only our purpose to have a service but to reflect upon the great motifs of the service. We shall, therefore, use a structure of common worship in which we have all participated whenever we have gone to church whether it be in Quaker meeting or Anglican Eucharist. After the enunciation of the immediate motif, we will reflect quietly upon it for a few minutes and then proceed. For prayer time, sit quietly and relax; there is not room to kneel. Those of you who are familiar with them, may join in the General Confession, the Lord's Prayer and the General Thanksgiving.

All worship begins with an announcement of the presence of the living God or an invocation of his presence.

The Lord is in his holy temple: let all the earth keep silence before him.

O worship the Lord in the beauty of holiness; let the whole earth stand in awe of him.

God is almighty. There is no God beside God, and there is no way that we can make God useful. We cannot harness his power to save America, western culture, or ourselves, except in accordance with his will. In his presence there is no alternative to seeing ourselves as we really are. The appearance of the living God amongst us drives us to our knees in repentance.

This is literally an age of life or death decisions. We shall decide whether we shall live or die as a world, as a culture; perhaps even whether we shall live or die physically. The young people whom we educate may die prematurely in brush-fire wars or they may be bereaved of their young ones. Who can say that we as Christians and as school people have been faithful, diligent, concerned, and loving enough in our vocation under God? Let us humbly confess our sins to almighty God.

Almighty and most merciful Father; We have erred, and strayed from thy ways like lost sheep. We have followed too much the devices and desires of our own hearts. We have offended against thy holy laws. We have left undone those things which we ought to have done; And we have done those things which we ought not to have done; And there is no health in us. But thou, O Lord, have mercy upon us, miserable offenders. Spare thou those, O God, who confess their faults. Restore thou those who are penitent; According to thy promises declared unto mankind in Christ Jesus our Lord. And grant, O most merciful Father, for his sake; That we may hereafter live a godly, righteous, and sober life, To the glory of thy holy Name. *Amen.*

We should not be able to bear the presence of this living and righteous God if we did not have the assurance of his grace and forgiveness most especially and intensively in his taking upon himself our human nature, and his reconciliation of the world unto himself in Christ. So now we hear God speaking authoritatively with the forgiveness of our sins.

Almighty God, the Father of our Lord Jesus Christ, who desireth not the death of a sinner, but rather that he may turn from his wickedness and live, hath given power, and commandment, to his Ministers to declare and pronounce to his people, being penitent, the Absolution and Remission of their sins. He pardoneth and absolveth all those who truly repent, and unfeignedly believe his holy Gospel.

Wherefore let us beseech him to grant us true repentance, and his Holy Spirit, that those things may please him which we do at this present; and that the rest of our life hereafter may be pure and holy; so that at the last we may come to his eternal joy; through Jesus Christ our Lord. *Amen.*

Our proper response is thanksgiving that is expressed in the prayer which our Lord has taught us to say.

Our Father, who are in heaven, Hallowed be thy Name. Thy kingdom come. Thy will be done, On earth as it is in heaven. Give us this day our daily bread. And forgive us our trespasses, As we forgive those who trespass against us. And lead us not into temptation, But deliver us from evil. For thine is the kingdom, and the power, and the glory, for ever and ever. Amen.

When we have met God and have been honest about our sins and have been forgiven, he edifies us by the reading from His word. Here beginneth the 23rd verse of the third chapter of St. Paul's Epistle to the Galatians:
Now before faith came, we were confined under the law, kept under restraint until faith should be revealed. So that the law was our custodian until Christ came, that we might be justified by faith. But now that faith has come, we are no longer under a custodian; for in Christ Jesus you are all sons of God, through faith. For as many of you as were baptized into Christ have put on Christ. There is neither Jew nor Greek, there is neither slave nor free, there is neither male nor female; for you are all one in Christ Jesus. And if you are Christ's, then you are Abraham's offspring, heirs according to promise.

Now, having been edified, we make our affirmation of faith. Unfortunately we cannot do that in a common tongue. I shall risk a paraphrase of a great creed: 'We believe in God the Father almighty, creator of heaven and earth. We believe in his life and action manifest in a full manhood united to

God reuniting an alienated world to himself. We believe in God's personal influence, his Holy Spirit, binding together the people of God here upon earth and forming and fashioning his life in that people. We believe that this great community of the Spirit is constituted by the citizens of God's final kingdom.'

When we have made our affirmation of faith then we may speak to God as children of God asking him for his mercy and help, for his strength and comfort, for his life and guidance, for his eternal presence among us.

Let us pray.

O God, from whom all holy desires, all good counsels, and all just works do proceed; Give unto thy servants that peace which the world cannot give; that our hearts may be set to obey thy commandments, and also that by thee, we, being defended from the fear of our enemies, may pass our time in rest and quietness; through the merits of Jesus Christ our Saviour. *Amen.*

Let us pray for all universities, colleges, and schools here represented, and particularly for the great public schools of this nation which know a double agony. The agony of facing a Herculean task with meager resources and the agony of integrating in the midst of their already great trials.

Almighty God, we beseech thee, with thy gracious favour to behold our universities, colleges and schools, that knowledge may be increased among us, and all good learning flourish and abound. Bless all who teach and all who learn; and grant that in humility of heart they may ever look unto thee, who art the fountain of all wisdom; through Jesus Christ our Lord. *Amen.*

Almighty God, who hast created man in thine own image; Grant us grace fearlessly to contend against evil, and to make no peace with oppression; and, that we may reverently use our freedom, help us to employ it in the maintenance of justice among men and nations, to the glory of thy holy Name; through Jesus Christ our Lord. *Amen.*

Now, let us offer our thanksgiving to God.

Almighty God, Father of all mercies, we, thine unworthy servants, do give thee most humble and hearty thanks for all thy goodness and loving-kindness to us, and to all men; We bless thee for our creation, preservation, and all the blessings of this life; but above all, for thine inestimable love in the redemption of the world by our Lord Jesus Christ; for the means of grace, and for the hope of glory. And, we beseech thee, give us that due sense of all thy mercies, that our hearts may be unfeignedly thankful; and that we show forth thy praise, not only with our lips, but in our lives, by giving up our selves to thy service, and by walking before thee in holiness and righteousness all our days; through Jesus Christ our Lord, to whom, with thee and the Holy Ghost, be all honour and glory, world without end. *Amen.*

The Grace of our Lord Jesus Christ, and the love of God, and the fellowship of the Holy Ghost, be with us all ever more. *Amen.*

SERVICE OF WORSHIP

Dr. Cleland

Let us pray.

O God, who art infinite, eternal and unchangeable; glorious in holiness; full of love and compassion, abundant in grace and truth; all thy works praise thee in all places of thy dominion; and thy glories are revealed in Jesus Christ thy Son. Wherefore we praise thee, Father, Son, and Holy Spirit, one God blessed forever. *Amen.*

O Lord, God, whose mercy is from everlasting to everlasting upon them that fear thee; hear our prayer of confession and for forgiveness. Forgive us our misusing of thy good gifts: the opportunity neglected, the half-truth accepted, the superficial judgment passed. Forgive us the unkind word, the unsympathetic heart, the false ambition and any unworthy purpose which has ruled our lives. We ask this in deep humility and, quiet confidence, because thou lovest us, and because we love thee more than we love our sins. *Amen.*

Our Father in heaven, give us thankful hearts as we gladly recall thy continued goodness to us. We thank thee for all thy gifts to thy children: for health, recreation, and refreshment; for interest in our work and power to do it; for all progress in things for which we care; for the companionship of fellow Christians; for all who have helped us with spiritual guidance or correction; for the unity with those who live in the spirit; for the pardon of our sins and the inspiration of thy presence. Thanks be to thee, O God, in Jesus Christ, our Lord. *Amen.*

Let us hear the Word of God in the Gospel According to St. John, the Fourth Chapter at the beginning:

'When therefore the Lord knew that the Pharisees had heard that Jesus was making and baptizing more disciples than John (although Jesus himself baptized not, but his disciples) he left Judaea, and departed again into Galilee. And he must needs pass through Samaria. So he cometh to a city of Samaria, called Sychar, near to the parcel of ground that Jacob gave to his son Joseph: and Jacob's well was there. Jesus therefore, being wearied with his journey, sat thus by the well. It was about the sixth hour. There cometh a woman of Samaria to draw water: Jesus saith unto her, Give me to drink. For his disciples were gone away into the city to buy food. The Samaritan woman therefore saith unto him, How is it that thou, being a Jew, askest drink of me, who am a Samaritan woman? (For Jews have no dealings with Samaritans.) Jesus answered and said unto her, If thou knewest the gift of God, and who it is that saith to thee, Give me to drink, thou wouldest have asked of him and he would have given thee living water. The woman saith unto him, Sir, thou hast nothing to draw with; and the well is deep: whence then hast thou that living water? Art thou greater than our father Jacob, who gave us the well and drank thereof himself, and his sons, and his cattle? Jesus answered and said unto her, Every one that drinketh of this water shall thirst again: but whosoever drinketh of the water that I shall give him shall never thirst; but the water that I shall give him shall become in him a well of water springing up unto eternal life. The woman saith unto him, Sir, give me the water, that I thirst not, neither come all the way hither to draw. Jesus saith unto her, Go, call thy husband, and come hither. The woman answered and said unto him, I have no husband. Jesus saith unto her, Thou saidst well, I have no husband: for thou hast had five husbands; and he who thou now hast is not thy husband: this hast thou said truly. The woman saith unto him, Sir, I perceive that thou art a prophet. Our father worshipped in this mountain, and ye say, that in Jerusalem is the place where men ought to worship. Jesus saith unto her, Woman, believe me, the hour cometh, when neither in this mountain, nor in Jerusalem, shall ye worship the Father. Ye worship that which ye know not: we worship that which we know; for salvation is from the Jews. But the hour cometh, and now is, when the true worshipper shall worship the Father in spirit and truth: for such doth the Father seek to be his worshippers. God is a spirit and they that worship him must worship him in spirit and truth. The woman saith unto him, I know that Messiah cometh (he that is called Christ): when he is come, he will declare unto us all things. Jesus saith unto her, I that speak unto thee am *he*.

'And upon this came his disciples; and they marvelled that he was speaking with a woman; yet no man said, What seekest thou? So the woman left her water-pot, and went away into the city, and saith to the people, Come, see a man who told me all things that *ever* I did: can this be the Christ?'

Let us pray. Let us offer unto God our prayers of inter-cession for the civil government and for the church.

O Lord, thou God of righteousness, who are the Lord of Lords; grant the guidance of thy Holy Spirit to our President and his cabinet, to the members of Congress and all in posi-tions of responsibility. May they never wrongly lead the na-tion through love of power, the desire to please, or unworthy ideals. May they always love righteousness and truth. So may thy name be held holy and magnified, to thy honor and to thy glory. *Amen.*

O God, our Shepherd, give to the Church a new vision

and a new charity, new wisdom and fresh understanding, the revival of her brightness and the renewal of her unity; that the eternal message of thy Son, undefiled by the traditions of men, may be hailed as the good news of the new age; through him who maketh all things new, even Jesus Christ, our Lord. *Amen.*

Now let us offer unto God our prayers of supplication for ourselves.

O God, who art the Truth and the Teacher of all who come to thee for light and guidance; bless us, a company of teachers who are met to worship thee. In times of doubt and questionings, when our belief is perplexed by new learning, new teaching, new thought; when our faith is strained by creeds and doctrines and mysteries beyond our understanding, give us the faithfulness of learners and the courage of believers in thee. Give us boldness to examine and faith to trust all truth; patience and insight to master difficulties; stability to hold fast our traditions with enlightened interpretations; to admit all fresh truth, and to combine it loyally and honestly with the old; through him, who is the truth, Jesus Christ, our Lord. *Amen.*

HANS HOFMANN:

CHRISTIAN REVELATION AND

THE INSIGHTS OF PSYCHOLOGY

THE REVEREND HANS HOFMANN brings to his teachings of Systematic Theology and Psychology of Religion at the Princeton Seminary preparation which was both thorough and diverse. He prepared for his degree in theology at the Universities of Basel and Zurich; for his degree in philosophy at the University of Paris; and for his diploma in psychoanalysis at the C. G. Jung Institute. Among his teachers in theology were Karl Barth, Emil Brunner and Rudolph Bultmann; in philosophy Karl Jaspers and Jean-Paul Sartre; in psychology C. G. Jung and Jean Piaget. Professor Hofmann's first book in English was published under the title *The Theology of Reinhold Niebuhr.*

CHRISTIAN REVELATION
AND THE
INSIGHTS OF PSYCHOLOGY

The phenomenon which we are facing today is that psychology and religion, to some extent, are brought together; but, we must remember that this is only 'to some extent.' Psychology is a scientific discipline and no substitute for religion. It shares with all sciences the phenomenological approach—that is to say, it is not interested in what is not or should be, but rather its concern is to describe what is. The heightened interest in psychology today has been aroused because of the new importance of its sister-discipline, psychiatry. As we know, psychiatry is a medical science which is devoted to the healing of emotional disturbances and mental disease. From this science has arisen the question of the exact nature of the relationship between religion and psychology.

I

It is significant, I think, that those who first discovered the depth of the human soul by trying to reach down into the unawareness inside man (depth psychology) were led by a Jew. Sigmund Freud resented the fact that he was Jewish. The same holds true for a man who is even more popular in the United States today. Former Rabbi Erich Fromm is an ardent, if not violent, exponent of Freudian psychoanalysis. Both Freud and Fromm have fought religion because they feel that religion does not help, but rather hinders, the free development of human personality. We may find this disturbing because these people have clinical facts against us, but we had better listen carefully to what they are saying, for their critiques may help us to understand our present-day religious problems.

Another interesting development today is the fact that two great men have arrived—one sooner than the other—at the conclusion that religion must bring together the various emphases and heritages of the many religions. The latest thought of Albert Schweitzer follows this line of theological syncretism (bringing together the best of all religions), and so does the thought of Arnold Toynbee. In the same book, in which he talks about the self-centeredness of man, he also talks about the relativity of the different religions. Says Toynbee, it is no longer important whether you are a Christian, a Buddhist, a Jew. It is much more important that whatever is real shall come alive for you.

This is reminiscent of the times of Jesus Christ. The ideal religion of the Hellenistic world was that which the individual formed for himself by drawing on the insights of various oriental mystery cults and the wisdom of Greek philosophy. In Rome, stood the Pantheon, a magnificent building dedicated to all the gods worshipped throughout the Roman Empire. We are really tolerant and true liberals, they said; it makes no difference which gods you happen to like best. It was rather embarrassing when they discovered that the Jews had no statue of their god to put in the Pantheon, in view of the fact that they would have been gracious enough to accept even him.

There was only one catch in the religious tolerance of Rome, and that was that all these gods had to be religious only. No mere god could make any contribution to the

political, social, or economic situation; this was the depart-
ment of the Divine Emperor. If you will recall what Dean
Cleland said last night, sharpening up what has already been
said by Herberg, that religion in our country today has
perhaps no purpose than to make us better Americans, you
will understand, for example, the piousness which generally
breaks out around election time.

The feeling is that one should have religion, but that it
should not be meaningful enough to make any trouble for
anyone. This is exactly the point where Freud realized that,
to many, their religion made no difference—whether it was
a religion of the strict, institutionalized sort or merely a personal belief or feeling. He felt that there was something
basically corrupt in this kind of religion—and rightly so.

Read the Gospel and discover for yourself how most of
Jesus' trouble arose. His greatest difficulties lay not in his
dealings with the black sheep of society. He had the most
trouble with the 'saints,' the wonderful, dignified, religious and political leaders of his time. He was not killed
by an unimportant fanatic. Rather, he was systematically
eliminated from the scene by the High Priest and the national leaders.

What Jesus really fought was the double arrogance of his
own fellow-Jews: on the one hand, the arrogance of those
who thought their religious duties quite fulfilled because
they went to the Temple and kept the Law; on the other,
the arrogance of those who could not comprehend that being
good means more than just doing good deeds. They and
we are like the young man in the Gospel who said, 'How
do I get to Heaven?' He knew and observed the Law, but
still he asked. Then Jesus said, 'All right, come and follow
Me.' But giving himself completely to something which he
could not control was not this young man's dish of tea. He
was sorry; and so was Jesus, for Jesus saw that the young
man had missed his chance for life.

II

What is it in religion which really matters? What matters in religion is not what we say about it or even what we do, but rather, what it means to us. Children are very sensitive to this. They watch us carefully, especially when we talk about religion. 'Why does he talk that way?' they want to know. And if they get the feeling that we talk that way just because we are paid for it, what happens then?

The question we must face is, simply, what does religion mean? Is religion a part of our over-all world-view? Or is it merely another cultural institution? If it is either of these, religion becomes an insult to the living God. This is where psychology puts us on the spot. Psychology tells us that if our religion is not alive in us, then it is not only dead but a stumbling block as well.

In our day, we find ourselves not knowing where to turn, especially in the field of politics. The entire Western world today really does not know which way to turn, so it puts on a big front; but behind that front, it is desperately seeking for some answer that would make sense. This is exactly the situation of adolescents. The sensitive front with which they come to school indicates that they wish to be regarded as adults. They are jealous of their privacy; they do not wish to be bossed around. But, behind all this, they want to find themselves, and to find themselves on their own. You may prepare some dish for them, of which they were very fond as children; but do not tell them to eat it. But just turn your back for a moment, and it will be gone.

Education which deals with personal religion in the period of adolescence can never be merely injected. We must leave off the 'mommy knows best' approach. If it comes from mommy, it is highly suspect anyway. Religion for the adolescent boy or girl cannot be something which they just *take*, and rightly so; yet, on the other hand, they are tremendously interested. How does one become a person? They read the biographies of great men, and wonder what magic ingredient is necessary for success.

The seeking of the young adolescent, as we see him in the prep school period, boils down to the one question, 'Now who am I anyway?' He is caught in a tension, because he still has to appear like somebody. He has one front for home; one for his teachers in school; one for his roommates and buddies; and another, just beginning to develop, for the time when he will be with friends of the opposite sex. This appears as the only way he can get along; but gradually it becomes more and more disturbing, as the boy or girl asks himself how all these different people can exist in one. And who is the one in whom they all exist? It would be folly to believe that young people believe in their own self-confidence. The good things that they, deep down, want to do, they can't do; the bad things, that they really hate, that is what they do.

'Miserable creature that I am,' as St. Paul summed it up. Our young people are discovering that life is overpowering. It is not only a problem of sex; Freud was deeply mistaken on this point. But if it is more than sex, what is it? The real problem of the adolescent is: how can I develop into a real person and still be popular and accepted, still be a good student, still be successful?

If, at this point, we resort to trickery with these boys and girls, we have failed them miserably. Jesus meant business when he said that some would have a millstone tied around the neck. If we try to present to them some simple formula for living and doing, if we resort to moralism, for instance, or if we represent religion in authoritarian terms, we have failed the young person, as well as having insulted the living God.

On the other hand, we may try to pass off their problems as unimportant. 'It's all part of growing up,' we say. 'I went through it all too.' But then they will look at what we are and say, 'God forbid!' And they will be right. If we really think we are any kind of example for our youth, we are seriously in error. Rather, the adolescent is encountering the basic problems of human life. Let us not make light of that! The adolescent is interested in gaining or losing his life, and he means business.

III

It is at this point that you may identify life with vitality. In this, psychology and religion are interrelated. They are related, exactly in the way presented by Dr. Cleland last night. I am in full agreement with his analysis of the contradiction between love and law.

During the time that he is in our classes, the adolescent finds out about law. There are two problems involved. One revolves about the fact that it is impossible to keep the law all the time. But St. Paul has said, 'If you miss one point, you miss the whole point of the law.' The adolescent knows this. If he trespasses anywhere, he has trespassed the meaning of the law. The other problem is: Is it so terribly exciting to keep the law anyway? Will keeping the law give anyone a kick out of life? The adolescent considers this carefully, for he knows that keeping the law means acceptance by others. If you are a law-breaker, you are out. This aids us in one of our favorite tricks. We point out the offender and say, 'He broke the law. Look at him; he did it.' And, of course, everyone looks, leaving the offender very much alone.

What about law? What about love? This is the time when they are beginning to find out about love, too. They want to know about Christian love (and not that other terrible love between people, which is a little too human for us). What then about the love of God? How terribly we caricature it! The love of God is just plain wonderful! It is completely selfless: He is giving all the time.

Now who could live that way? Nobody. Not even you. So why present it this way to young people? Our presentation sounds as unnatural as the tape recording of a speech. And why does it sound this way? Because it really does not come from the heart. Yet if anything should come from the heart, it is love. Again psychology makes something clear to us. We must stop talking about love as if we could love; we just cannot.

It is very significant to note how we talk about making love. We mean mere sex play. The simple fact is that we cannot 'make' love; we cannot love on our own. But neither can we live without love. In this predicament, psychology cannot help us. I submit that psychology and psychoanalysis are tremendously helpful in bringing out our real problems, but no psychology can give us life or teach us how to love.

IV

Today, psychiatrists are calling for ministers who have a realistic understanding of the relationship between life and religious faith and who are able to communicate this understanding in vital ways. The psychiatrists have no trouble in being utterly realistic; their difficulty lies in the limitations to which a science is always subjected. A psychiatrist cannot concern himself with the ultimate 'why' and 'how.'

Let us return to the question of love. It is nonsense for us to tell our boys and girls, 'You just happen to be here.' Interestingly enough, the Bible tells us that man is created for a specific reason and with a special intention. Man is not just a tank which is going to be filled. The truth is that this boy and this girl are here because of love. To put it bluntly, if two people were not most intimately interrelated, we would have no children. This is not a biological function of man. This is the meaning of man. *Genesis* tells us that God has created man. Why? Because God, being love, wants to express himself lovingly to somebody who then would have the ability to respond to him. That is manhood—the ability to respond to love.

Do you know what it means to say that God has created man so that he can face him? The image of God is not something that we have in ourselves or once had. The image of God is our functional and intentional position in which the Creator has placed us. Namely, it is to be God's own counterpart, responding to his love with our love. Here we have arrived at the point where psychology gets stuck.

Psychology knows we need love, but it does not know where love comes from. Man is created to be with God. The only difference between the human and all other animals is that man can recognize himself as somebody who responds or who has the ability to respond. Manhood depends on our ability to respond to the love that addresses itself to us. That is the aim of child psychology in a nutshell.

Whenever a child is maladjusted, whenever a child gives trouble, he really does not know what he is because he was never fully loved; and therefore he could not fully respond to love. What does love mean? That someone can say to you, 'I am so interested in you that I want the best for you,' or 'I am happy for your good fortune because you are so worthwhile to me that I want the best for you.' Who understands this feeling more than a child? Love a child, and you can do anything with him. You can even be harsh with him. A child will take anything which he knows comes out of love. Your demands become the possibility for the child to express what he feels for the one who loved him first. This is the meaning of the whole Bible; and, as Dr. Cleland said, 'That comes long before law.' Look at the Covenant in the Old Testament. It is nothing more than a partnership between God and man in love.

V

Now let us look at the Ten Commandments. I have asked students in Princeton how the Ten Commandments begin, and they answered, 'Thou shalt, and thou shalt not.' This is not true. Do you know how they begin? God says, 'I am your God, who brings you out of the house of slavery and this is *how* you are set free—set free from chasing other gods; set free from having idols; set free from lusting after someone else's goods; set free from the compulsion to build yourself up at the expense of God or other men.'

Why don't we teach children the Law as it is meant. That is, as a test case. We are free and human, not because of man but because of God. Love may then express itself through the channels of the Law. But, love comes first. The Law is merely a possibility to express and to respond to love.

But it is hard for us to explain love to our children. I am sorry to say that love is one of the things we just don't understand. We think of love as a vague emotional sentimentality. If you have to tell your school children that you love them, then you certainly do not. Love is not something which is talked about. Do not go home thinking that I have given you some magic formula. 'Love takes care of everything.' This is not so; love is no formula. Love is the *possible* way in which lives may be related to each other, and therefore love is creative. This is why you can never substitute any religious trickery for love; yet love can use all the channels of religious expression.

For example, sometimes we think that we must have elaborate and special religious programs to attract the interest of our children. For a while they may like this; then they may dislike it intensely. We cannot depend on the ever changing tastes of children. But love makes us flexible enough to put up with this. As the Bible puts it, love sets us free. Where love unites, all is good; where it does not unite, there is separation and evil.

Sin is not just something wrong you did (but probably enjoyed anway). Sin is not so simple. Sin is what separates us from the source of life and from the One with whom you can live only in love. Jesus knew what sin is. He told the Jews that their Temple worship was not enough, that they had to enter a love-relationship with God.

VI

How much of our religion is merely a hiding behind bushes from God and our fellow men? What is the meaning of the Fall of Man? Man wanted to know what is good and evil, on his own. I do not call this bad; this is a religious drive. But sin creeps in where a man thinks, 'If I find out all by my self; then I will be good, I will be a saint.' So we have to find out what is good and what is evil. But we look at ourselves and others, finding that others are different from us. Who is the right one? So we cover ourselves up. This is what the Bible means by 'clothing themselves.' We often do this with our children. Some days we simply feel like hell—and hell, in the sense of being isolated, utterly alone. But in spite of our feeling miserable, we have to go to our classes. So we put on a specially contrived smile; and if the headmaster asks us how we feel, we say, 'Fine.'

Fine. To say this, is death. Why? Because it is a denial of love. That is, we do not believe that God loves us enough so that we dare to be before all the world exactly what we are inside. This is why, when God comes to seek him out, we find Adam hiding behind the bushes. To God's call, Adam replies, I am just not worthy to come before thee. How worthy are any of us? In religion, legalism is man's attempt to make himself worthy enough to come before God and to receive God's good gifts. God, I stopped smoking, now please take care of my grades. And it is exactly here, in legalism where life is castrated and petrified.

But you can never make something of yourself by yourself or find out who you are on your own. Nor will you find out by reading volumes on psychology. For one thing, all these books are not written just for you; that is the trouble with them. You, and everyone else, are unique. You dare not identify your own problems exactly with some case you are reading in Freud; you may discover that the case you are reading about ends in incurable schizophrenia.

We laugh at this, but isn't this the way we often try to use psychology. We regard it as a miraculous cure-all. 'If you only had the money for a psychiatrist then everything would be all right.' How wrong!

Psychology calls for one thing: *the courage to be.* We must go out in the world the way we are; that is the way we must find ourselves. This is the kind of experience the Bible points us to. Paul does not say that he discovered the power of positive thinking, after which things just got better and better. Rather, Paul says, 'Verily, we are like sheep before the slaughter. We are persecuted. We are laughed at, but we are not annihilated, we are not destroyed by it.' We live, the prey neither of our self-accusations nor the accusation around us. This is the courage to be. This is the freedom to live.

How does this come? This does not come through the practice of religion nor of psychology either. It can only come about where God, himself, says to you, 'You are all right for me; and I give my own life'—God's own life— 'through death and hell, that you may succeed in your life.' It is unbelievable to know that God is always following us with love. This love is the vitality which is spoken of in psychology; it is what is meant by justification by faith in theology. No matter who accuses you or who is against you, you are free to grow daily into the realization of the love of

God. Thus you will come to maturity; and maturity is that which is necessary for us to be able to proclaim the good news about God.

VII

We talk much too early. Dr. Cleland is right about that. But we have to talk. How should we do it? Who am I to say anything? If you ask this question, you are already lost. You may be anything from a louse to a saint; it doesn't matter. If you speak in your own name, in the name of your religion, or in the name of your morality—if you speak for yourself, shut up. But, if you come to your young people, saying that God may speak through you; then something will happen. Then, perhaps for the first time, your children will realize that you are not God nor even the Pope, but that you don't have to be either. You, the teacher, become someone who can help your students toward the maturity which comes only from God. Religious maturity means that we recognize everything short of God as functional. Thus, God can use your maturity to spread his love which is life.

But there will still be growth out of maturity. The best means for this are reminiscent of the stitches used in medicine, which do not have to be removed because they are gradually absorbed by the organism. Growth out of maturity means that whatever is used in your life is gradually absorbed and changed by this one Life which is dynamic, and which takes into its dynamic self expression all of you, so that you become alive. So you will become psychologically and theologically sound, and also, you will live by love, which is forgiveness.

At the end of the day, God will not ask you how many mistakes you made in your classes. If he were to do that, we would all be sunk. But God will ask you how much of his love came through your life and how much forgiveness. And if you do not know forgiveness in your own life, you cannot forgive either. Without forgiveness, no love is possible.

How much do you live by this love of God? Look at the gospel story of the man left beside the road to die. All the religious officials passed by on the other side. They did not have time to do anything for him; they were already late for a meeting at the Temple. Then along comes a dubious person, a half-breed Jew (we might have called him a Negro); he was the only one who had the time or the love to help.

We always tell this story as if the man who helped the sick man was just wonderful. But what does the Bible say? It bids us turn our attention to the one who was hurt. He is the one who gave them a chance to experience in service what love means.

Look at the prostitute, to whom Jesus said, 'Where is your husband?' When she said, 'I do not have one,' Jesus replied, 'That is right; and the man you live with is not your husband either.' If we were to take this attitude with people, most of them would tell us to mind our own business, but what did this woman do? She ran to the town, telling everyone that she had met the Messiah. Why? Because she knew he was being critical out of love.

St. Augustine says, 'Love, and do what you want.' It is indeed a terrifying statement—if one does not know what love means.

SERVICE OF WORSHIP

Dr. Hofmann

Let us pray.

God our Father, we come before thee, not on our own merits. We come before thee for thou hast called us and hast called us in love. Thou knowest us, our hearts and minds, our soul and our flesh. There is not one moment in our days when thou art not with us. We thank thee that thou knowing us, lovest us. That thy knowing of us will bring us again into renewal of our life. Come with thy Holy Spirit, thy breath of life. O come, Creator Spirit, and fill us again. We shall go out from here, back into these places where we labor and where we doubt; where we suffer, and where we fall. Grant us, we beseech thee, that all that is ours, all that burdens our hearts and minds, known and unknown, confessed and hidden; be it not only revealed before thy heart of love, but taken from us. Take us again into thy hands; make us living signposts of thy grace; and open our hearts and minds that the written word may become a living word. Speak this through the mouth of thy servant, to all of us, that thy words may go out and overcome the world evermore. *Amen.*

The Gospel According to St. Matthew reads as follows: [Jesus Christ appears on the day of ascension before his disciples] 'And when they saw him, they worshipped him; but some doubted. And Jesus came and said to them, "All authority in heaven and on earth has been given to me. Go, therefore, and make disciples of all nations, baptizing them in the name of the Father and of the Son and of the Holy Spirit, teaching them to observe all that I have commanded you; and lo, I am with you always, to the close of the age." '

The Gospel account gives a surprisingly realistic picture of human nature. Although we were not disciples, we know that the reaction of the disciples to the risen Christ is our own: we worship him, but some doubt. This doubt does not so much concern the historical Jesus but the living Gòd. But the Gospel does not condemn those who doubt the living Lord. Rather, it suggests a way in which all doubts may be overruled, when Jesus says, 'All authority in heaven and earth has been given to me.'

Can we learn together that we need his help? That we need his help not only in the chapel services, not only in classes, or as we pray; but when we read the papers or deal with young people so far from Galilee? When we doubt, could we remember that he has power above Mr. Khrushchev and above the White House, too? Can we learn to go about our daily life in the presence of a victorious Lord, who reigns supreme in love—God's love in Jesus Christ, which did and which will surely overcome the world? Can we in our weakness and failure be witnesses of this victory? Of this man who is ever with us, in love? Even critically in love, so that all that is phony about us will be burnt up in the fire of his presence and all that is true and real will be fortified.

He does have the power, and he is with us. But here does not end the lesson of the evening. It also includes the commission to go out into all nations, bringing them into baptism and victory, that they may die with Christ to their own illusions and rise with Christ in life everlasting. Go and talk with them about all that Jesus Christ has brought to us. Talk so that by this conversation, student and faculty alike, may grow into the full stature of true manhood which is in Jesus Christ, who in washing the feet of his disciples showed us the kind of lord he is. What we do will be judged by this: if it is the living proclamation of the joyful life and the goodness of our Lord and Master.

Let us pray.

Father, we thank thee for the gift of life. We do not understand; we cannot grasp thee; we cannot witness on our own. We know this and we confess it before thee. Keep us from seeking to be thy servants on our own. Deliver us from delusions of grandeur. Come, O Father, and spread again among us, thy life. O come, and fulfill this world according to thy promise. Come, O Lord Jesus, quickly. We ask this since we know that we are weak. We ask this, since through our weakness thy strength may be glorified, through Jesus Christ our Lord. *Amen.*

ALBERT T. MOLLEGEN:

THE MEANING OF LOVE IN
CHRISTIAN THOUGHT

THE REVEREND ALBERT T. MOLLEGEN is the Professor of New Testament Language and Literature at the Protestant Episcopal Theological Seminary in Alexandria, Virginia. He was educated, first, in electrical engineering at Mississippi State College; later, in theology at the Virginia Seminary, where he now lectures, and at the Union Theological Seminary in New York. The University of the South has honored him with the degree of Doctor of Divinity. He founded and now lectures in a theological college for lay persons in Washington, D. C., which has become a center for relating Christianity to psychiatry, modern art, and contemporary social, political, and economic problems. In addition, he lectures during the summer at the Union Seminary on Theology and Ethics, and writes for various publications on religious subjects.

THE MEANING OF LOVE IN CHRISTIAN THOUGHT

My task has been described as that of synthesizing what is going on in this conference. Since that word sounds as if something synthetic is to happen, perhaps, you'll let me substitute the word 'correlate.'

I

The first correlation that I would like to make is a semantic one. Dr. Cleland spoke in terms of law and faith, and Dr. Hofmann spoke in terms of law and love. There is no essential difference, however, in their point of view. Dr. Cleland was speaking 'justification by faith' language. This language stems directly from the Epistles of St. Paul, where faith is the inclusive word that describes the total human response to God in Christ reconciling the world unto himself. The coming of Christ, and the act of reconciliation which is the whole life and ministry of Christ centering in his death and resurrection, is spoken of by St. Paul as stemming from the divine grace, the divine favor of God towards man, or the love of God, commending itself to us. While we were yet sinners, Christ died for us. That language speaks of the downward sweep of the divine love focusing concretely in the living historical personality of Christ. Who he is and what he did evokes an answering response: *faith*. This is first of all a reception of that love; secondly, an act of absolute committal to the God; and, thirdly, a trustful throwing of oneself into the hands of that God. Faith is a giving of self to God, in return for God's gift of Himself to us in Christ. Now, in that context, faith is the human response which sets us within the whole ongoing life of God. Obedience to law, as it is newly understood, is the inevitable result.

When I caught the train to come to Atlantic City, I had to have some faith that the Pennsylvania Railroad was going to take me to North Philadelphia and to Atlantic City. The faith-act on my part was simply to board the train and to put my reliance in the Pennsylvania Railroad. Thus, too, in justification by faith theology (St. Paul's), faith is that response to the divine love which ties us in into the whole ongoing love of God, so that we go where God goes; and, since God goes out in love for that other, we, who are tied into his life by faith, move with him outward in love towards the other. In other words, faith throws us into a right relationship with God, and through this right relationship the whole power of the divine personal influence flows. Another name for God's forthgoing personal influence is Holy Spirit.

God is the Holy Spirit, and love of neighbor is the fruit of the Divine Spirit, the Holy Spirit, the Spirit of Christ working in us. Therefore, faith expresses itself in obedience to law as love—the fruit of the Holy Spirit.

Now Dr. Hofmann, on the other hand, was speaking in the terms of Catholic and 'Johannine' language. He switched from his native Protestant theological language, and I will tell you why he did so: Because he was speaking not only the language of St. John, (particularly as we find it in the epistles); but also the language of St. Augustine and of medieval Catholicism—they all use *love* instead of *faith*. In this context, love is the ground of the forthgoing action of

God towards man in the person of Jesus; but love is also the response by which man receives that divine love. So that, instead of faith as man's attitude toward God, love is the word describing the response to the divine love. Faith, in this theological language, is preliminary to love toward God. St. John, in the first epistle bearing his name, says that Christians love God because God first loved us in Christ Jesus and him crucified. We love him (God) because he first loved us.

Love, therefore, on man's part (insomuch as it moves toward God) is evoked or elicited by the divine love. Love begets love. The divine love begets the human response of love; and, then, since the God whom we love loves every other, we who love God must also love God's other children. So, love, is also the outgoing moral action with its inner motivation that composes the heart of Christian ethics.

So, on the Catholic side—in the language of St. Thomas, St. Augustine, and St. John—love is used for all a Christian's relations. The divine love begets the human love, which moves back to its God, and outward to the neighbor as Christian love. It moves outward to others in the mission of the Church, and as Christian concern for the welfare of others.

Now, why did the Swiss Reformed theologian use the language of love which is historically the language of Catholicism? This is because he has been trained in modern psychology and has been in continuous conversation with modern psychotherapy—with psychiatrists and those who do intensive psychotherapy, the psychoanalysts. The reason I know this is that I have been increasingly pushed into using the love language in similar dialogues. Psychiatrists are increasingly using the language of love.

II

Let us now speak about correlation between theology, as

represented by the two earlier speakers, and psychology and psychotherapy as Dr. Hofmann spoke of them and as we have heard them referred to in many of our group discussions, especially the panel discussions of last night. Psychology, insomuch as it is a science, is like every other science. In and of itself, it is without morality or without value. It is, as Dr. Hofmann said, 'phenomenological.' It is utterly descriptive. But Christianity is concerned with the therapeutic art which is informed by the science. We are interested in the science because it helps to understand and heal persons. I use heal here in the widest sense.

Now, the language of the psychoanalysts—or the psychiatrists (the psychotherapists)—may vary some. I think we will all agree that they understand man through the combination of their scientific knowledge and their concern for man. Their concern for man and their doctrine of man may come out of a humanistic tradition or from a Christian commitment—Roman Catholic or Protestant. Whatever their religious or philosophical commitment, it gives them a concern for men and a doctrine of man, that is not empirical. Their therapy is never purely scientific. It is an art based upon science and informed and motivated by their commitments, secular humanistic or profoundly religious. On the whole, I would say that most of the psychoanalysts whom I know in Washington—and I know a good many of them—would classify as existentialists, with a deep respect for all forms of religion, particularly for Western religions, Judaism and Christianity; but, some of them are baptized church people.

Now our concern in this conference is with the therapeutic art as it is informed by an understanding and concern for man. It is psychotherapy which is able to speak about man's problem as being primarily and basically a love problem, and is able to speak about therapy as a context in which love can emerge in human relationships. At times, however, Reformation language is used. I remember hearing Dr. Edith Weigert, an able Washington psychoanalyst, say after a meeting of Continental and American psychoanalysts some years ago, that they had developed their own particular directions in isolation from each other for so long that they had difficulty in communicating; that the only thing that they could immediately and clearly agree upon was a common task to produce trust in man. Trust is the language of faith on the one hand, and the language of love on the other. If I had to give one single word to describe what Martin Luther meant by faith in the great Reformation slogan 'by faith alone,' I would use the English word, 'trust.' That would be the nearest single word that would translate what he meant by 'faith.'

My point is simple. Psychiatrists are a group of humanistic healers of the human psyche, who have diagnosed man's problem as essentially and basically a love problem. They understand their healing art as being that which is conducive to the emergence of love in human life. Therefore, it is inevitable that any of us who try to correlate Christianity and psychotherapy shall drift towards the love language. It is a common language for both theologians and psychotherapists.

III

The fact that we use a common language does not mean there is not great difficulty in understanding each other. Misunderstandings exist on both sides. Nor does it mean that once the misunderstandings have been cleared up that we find ourselves immediately in agreement. This is not true.

I have been a member of a seminar of theologians and psychoanalysts that meets one full evening every month. We are in our sixth year, and I think none of us would say that we have arrived at a complete correlation of the two points of view. Rather, there is a continuous dynamic tension in the dialogue. Both sides are conditioned, each by the other, to the great benefit and health of both. It is not an easy correlation.

The crux of the dilemma lies in the meaning of the word love itself. The crux of the issue lies in the meaning of self-fulfillment. Even when misunderstandings are cleared up and language is translated back and forth by each side, it still appears to the humanistic psychotherapists that Christianity mutilates the human ego. They have questions, therefore, about sacrifice, about Christian self-sacrifice. The central symbol of Christianity is a cross on which a young man lays down his life. His life is cut off. One aspect of this is that he is not even able to carry out his filial responsibility to his mother. His whole life is cut off, frustrated. Both, the symbols of Christianity (the language of Christianity) and the distorted Christianity of the patients whom these psychiatrists treat, leads them to understand Christianity as being fundamentally an enemy of self-fulfillment. Most psychiatrists, however, have passed beyond this point in their questioning because they know there is ambiguity in the word 'self'. Who is the 'self' in self-fulfillment?

Now, I should like to speak on this because it is a fundamental point, not only for the conversation between psychotherapists and Christians, but also, I think, for any kind of dealing with teenagers. I do not think that you will be received with enthusiasm if you approach teenagers with a request to abrogate their selfhood. At their age they are particularly seeking self-fulfillment, and they are in the peculiar dilemma of not knowing what that self is which needs fulfillment. That dilemma has been excellently described by Dr. Hofmann.

This, then, has importance not only for the dialogue between psychoanalysts and theologians, but also for the conversation between adults and teenagers, whether the adults be religious leaders or psychotherapists, parents or prep-school teachers.

IV

I should like, at some length and with some care, to exposit by paraphrase the great solution to this problem given by St. Bernard of Clairveaux. (There is a kind of anti-intellectualism in our culture that thinks that anybody who quotes anybody who wrote before 1900 is an impractical egghead. This attitude shuts us off from a great deal of profound thinking and from great Christian and human wisdom.) I shall paraphrase St. Bernard because his language is medieval, but in doing so, I shall not misrepresent him.

St. Bernard observes that everyone starts out loving himself. We love ourselves for our self's sake. In other words, the emergence of human consciousness in the infant is very soon met by the egocentric thrust of other people. Self-fulfillment, self-grasping, self-concern on the part of those in the child's environment meets with his own self-centeredness— the self-love that is necessary for him to survive—and enhances it.

This radical self-centeredness of all human nature is, what Christianity calls, 'original sin.' In extraordinarily righteous people, egocentricity expresses itself in self-righteousness. Original sin has nothing to do with the moral level upon which it appears. It appears on every moral level. You can never get rid of it by striving for moral goodness, because when you attain this moral goodness, you only have original sin expressing itself as self-righteousness.

Every man, St. Bernard says, begins by loving himself for self's-sake. Of course, he means fallen men, sinful men, the world as you see it—or in modern philosophical language, he means, existential man, man as he exists. For existentialism uses the word 'existence' and the phrase 'existential situation' to mean what we Christians mean by the mythical symbol 'fallen world.' By the fall we do not mean something that happened a long time ago in the garden of Eden. It describes our situation in relation to what we ought to be.

Then, says St. Bernard, no man is fool enough to think that he can make his love of self for self's-sake really stand up in the universe. He is not powerful enough for one thing. In ultimate and dramatic terms, he can not stay the hand of death. Self-love is finally frustrated by death, and every man knows this. From a very early period in our lives, we are aware that we must die. This is one of the clearest manifestations of our inescapable creatureliness. Nature is out to kill us and nature will succeed. We learn this long before we go near a biology classroom, but this is only an ultimate expression of the fact that man can not make his selfish self-love stand up.

So, St. Bernard says, man loves God for self's sake. On the whole, this is pagan religion when the attempt is made to bribe God, or cajole him, or flatter him, or persuade him to be on our side—to love God for self's-sake: To love God to save American culture or American capitalism; or to love God to establish some form of socialism that we believe in; to love God in order that we might pass our prep school examinations. In one of our discussion groups, we heard the story of the boy who was disillusioned in his Christian faith because in three successive years, in a crisis with a particular course, he had prayed to pass his examination. He had passed them the first two years, and the third year God let him down. He lost his faith. God had got tired of helping him pass his high school examinations.

Please do not misunderstand what I am saying. I am saying that it is a pagan religion which loves God for self's-sake, but, I am not saying that you should not indulge in pagan religion. You should, if you are pagan; and, let me frankly say, there is much really deep paganism in me.

To go into the presence of God where your meeting with God is informed by your deepest desires is to have a real encounter with God—and I am not condemning this at all; I am simply describing it. We therefore move out of love of self for self's sake into love of God for our self's sake. We appeal to God from our weakness or we appeal to God as if he were selfish. Do you remember what Moses used to say to God? 'Now, you cannot destroy your chosen people. Think of what the Gentiles will think of you if you do this.'

The whole effort is to persuade or to coerce God to get behind us. This is idolatry. It is to impose our image, the image of a particular race, of a particular culture, a particular economic system, of a particular magnified individual, upon God; and to identify some creaturely value with the divine; or put it another way, to deify some creaturely being, race, culture, nation, or self. This is idolatry. Where, therefore, as Dr. Cleland said, men worship the pagan gods, the false gods, they often do it under the theological and ritualistic symbols of the true God. When the pre-exilic prophets fought Baalism, their people were not necessarily overtly confessing Baalism. They were practicing Baalism in the guise of Yahwism. It was Baal whom they worshipped, but they worshipped him under the name of Yahweh.

To continue the thought of St. Bernard. When God enters the picture, when we learn to love God for self's sake, we are, at least, admitting our creatureliness, our need for God, and God can do something with this situation. St. Bernard is thinking, of course, of that mighty history of revelation which the Bible records, where God reveals himself to and through Abraham, Isaac, Jacob, Moses, Elijah, Amos, Hosea, Micah, Jeremiah, John the Baptist, and then, finally and fully, in Christ Jesus. When God enters the picture, then we may learn to love God for God's sake.

To love God for God's sake is the third stage of love, and it is the third stage of the history of religion. It is effected by the mighty action of God in Christ Jesus, whereby the divine love evokes from us a love towards God which we could not give by will power, which we could in no way produce in or by ourselves. Our love is simply elicited, evoked from us by the concrete striking in of God's love in and through Christ. 'We love him because he first loved us,' St. John said.

By God's action we come to love God for God's sake. Then, declares St. Bernard, and then alone 'can we love self for God's sake.' The love of self for God's sake, he says, is perfectly exemplified in the life of our Lord. In this historical first-century Jew, says St. Bernard, we have the perfect expression of a humanity which loved itself for God's sake.

Let us see what St. Bernard meant by this. Love of self is manifested very clearly in self preservation in maintaining oneself. Jesus didn't throw his life away in a foolhardy way. He took very good care of his life. He could have died in Galilee, executed by Herod Antipas. John the Baptist did. Instead, he evaded this death. He left Galilee and traveled incognito in the Phoenician country. Why—because he was selfish? Oh, no. Because he was still of more use to God alive than dead, he saved his life for God's sake. There came a time, however, in Jesus' ministry when the growth in the relationship between him and his disciples, and the development of the issues between himself and ecclesiastical and civil authorities of his time made him of more use to God dead than alive. There came a time when that which he could not effect by his life, he could effect by his death. There came a time when the whole great work which he came to do, could be done in no other way than by the Cross. So, when that time came, he gave his life in death. He gave it to God in the divine service, a perfect sacrifice; and he gave his life for man, reconciling the world unto God.

You see, he loved himself for God's sake, and he saved himself when he was of use to God alive, and he gave himself in death when he was of use to God in death. He loved himself for God's sake.

Look at the meaning of the word 'self' in these four stages of love, and, indeed, look at the meaning of love in these four stages of love. When we talk about self-negations, self-sacrifice, and when we talk about self-fulfillment, what self are we talking about? The self which loves itself for self's sake must be negated. The self that loves God for selfish ends must be negated. The self that loves God for God's sake must still learn to love self for God's sake. Only when we understand this, can we talk about self-fulfillment either to the psychotherapists who are not Christians, or to teenagers. Everything depends on what self is fulfilling itself. If you tell raw, unconverted, unredeemed teenagers that Christianity is self-fulfillment, this may only mean to them that the church has Elvis Presley records in the parish hall.

V

Now, let us try to correlate what we have said with the teenage world as we see it phenomenologically. This is not a depth analysis of the teenage situation, but, as we see them phenomenologically. On the whole, they speak the language of St. Augustine and of psychoanalysis, the language of love. They know the language of love, and they use it very casually of almost everything. 'I love Elvis Presley' meaning, I love his music. 'I love jitterbugging; I love ice cream; I love green curtains; I love John; I love my school; I love my parents; I love God; I love tennis; I love swimming; I love the beach.' It is the language of love, used quite casually. Teenagers know in a dark way that they do not love John and their parents with the same kind of love and with the same intensity as they love ice cream and tennis. They know there is some difference, but they are awfully cloudy and forget about these differences because they really do not know yet what is the nature of love. They are ready to learn from St. Augustine. Please do not misunderstand me. I do not mean you should stand up and read *The City of God* to them. St.

Augustine, as a Christian, sees life as being one great structure of love, in which everything participates: the inanimate world, the rocks, the soil, the rivers, planets; the vegetable world, the botanical world; the animal world—everything from snakes to elephants; the human world; and the divine world. God, man, animals, vegetables, and the inanimate. All of this participates in a great structure of love. It is created and maintained by the divine love. This is the Christian doctrine of creation, which is the answer to the question, 'What are you doing here?' Now, by 'here' I do not mean at this conference or at your prep schools—I mean rather this very embarrassing predicament of being a funny kind of rational animal stuck on a planet in a solar system which is a part of an infinite universe. What are you doing 'hanging out there?' The Christian doctrine of creation is not primarily a doctrine about something that happened a long time ago. It addresses the present and states that the only excuse for existence and for existing is that God wanted something other than himself upon which to bestow his love. You live by grace, by love. Whether you know it or not, you are sustained by it, you eat it, you breathe it. The whole thing is a great structure of love. Nothing would be, if it were not for the divine love.

In this great structure of love, says St. Augustine who called it 'the order of love', man was intended to love on three levels and in four directions. He was made to respond to God's love, to love God 'firstly and foremostly.' That is to love in the direction that is above himself: to love God. 'Thou shall love the Lord thy God with all thy psychosomatic being,' Jesus says; 'And again, seek ye first the kingship (the kingdom) of God, and everything else shall be added to you.'

So, man was made to love above himself, to love God. But he was made also to love on the level of himself in two directions: 'Love thy neighbor as thyself.' Two directions, one level, the human level; and here, you see the whole problem of self-love is solved, because the self that is commanded to love the self, is the self which has already been commanded to love God first. You cannot trust self-love unless you love God first; nor can you trust anybody to love his neighbor unless he loves God first, because if you love your neighbor as if you were that neighbor's God, then your love for him is destructive. In one way or another you will inevitably think you are his God, unless you have a God that you know is his God, a God whose place in his life you will not usurp.

All sin is, at one and the same time, a pretending to be God on the one hand, and a tyrant over others on the other hand. This is the classical Christian doctrine of sin. It is put mythically in the fall of the great angel Satan, who sought to dethrone God.

So, man was made to love God above himself, to love on the level of himself—to love his neighbor and to love himself; and he was made to love on the level below—to love the animal world, the vegetable world, and the inanimate world. Each order has its proper love, that which is due to each order. One should not love a horse as much as one should love a human being—even if one lives in Upperville, Virginia.

Now, says St. Augustine, the order of love has fallen into disorder. Man does not love in an orderly way, he loves inordinately, in a disorderly way; and so, life is in conflict, in strife. Why has everything fallen into disorder? Because we are alienated from God. Man has cut himself away from God. He refused to receive the love of God. He denied God the response of love. He no longer could worship. He could go to church and say prayers, but he could no longer worship God; and since he could no longer love God which is the central reason for his existence, then this vacuum in his selfhood, this unfulfilled thing that could only be satisfied by God, this deep thirst for God, is expressed in a relationship with something other than God.

And this *he* is we. We love some creature of God with a love that should go only to God. We are idolators. We deify our human systems, our values, our success, and culture. Because we must love God and because we deny the true God, we love a god of our own making. We deify a creature, and when we love a creature with a love that ought to go only to God, then the whole structure of love is bent and twisted. It is like a beautiful face in rubber. We reach out and pull the nose, thus distorting the whole face. It is a twisted world, because we do not love God.

In this disorder of love we may love beneath man, with the love that ought to go to man; we may love the gathering of physical things; we may love power more than we love man. Says St. Augustine, 'Man is what he loves as God.' If we love something as God that is not God, we become like that. Every man is like that which he loves most. By disordered love we are pulled out of our true selfhood, the selfhood that God made with its fulfillment that God intended. We have been distorted, shaped, and formed by the image of that which we love as God, made false by the falseness of our false love, our inordinate love.

Now, psychoanalysis and the Law agree, 'Thou shalt love.' St. Augustine agrees, 'Thou shalt love.' According to what the psychoanalyst is religiously, he will agree or disagree with, 'Thou shalt love the Lord thy God.' God will be in the picture or not. That is entirely a matter of the religious and philosophical outlook of the analyst. There is nothing about psychoanalysis which has anything to say about the validity of religion.

Let me tell you the story of a friend of mine, an East Indian Christian converted in his adulthood, a brilliant man, who was undergoing psychoanalysis with another friend of mine, who has an agnostic, secular-humanist in his outlook. At one point in his analysis the East Indian told the story of his conversion, which was a violent conversion. The analyst

said to him, 'Mr. So and So, you have described a very neurotic experience.' He said, 'Of course, I'm a neurotic, that is
why I am here having an analysis. Inevitably my neuroticism
would distort my religious experience.' The psychiatrist said,
'That is not quite what I meant.' He replied, 'Oh, you mean
that God is the projection of my neurotic needs? If you tell
me this, this is in the realm of philosophy and theology; and
I'll tell you, your lack of God is the projection of your neurotic needs. Now, let's get on with the analysis.'

There is nothing, nothing whatever, about either the
science, or the art, of psychology or psychiatry that says anything about any values. Individual psychoanalysts may be
religious or non-religious—they make their own commitments, but this is true also of physicists and bankers. The fact
that they are analysts does not mean that they are more philo-
sophically profound than was Henry Ford a great bringer of
peace in World War I because he was a great industrialist.
(You remember that peace ship he sent?) We oddly transfer
authority from one field to another. But psychotherapy does
speak the language of love; the teenager speaks the language
of love; and the Christian tradition can speak the language
of love, and emphatically does so on one side of its tradition.

If we are to make the child see this Christian order of love,
then we must quit telling him that his relationship to God is
something which comes in disguise. The Christian religion
is really expressed only in human relationships. Christianity
is irrevocably, firstly and foremostly, grounded in God, and
there is no other way to know God except by his self-dis-
closure (his revelation). There is nothing esoteric about the
fact of revelation. I can say about every one of you that you
are unknowable save by your revelation. There is absolutely
no way for me to know you unless you reveal yourself to me.
I may know a lot about you from the outside—say sociologi-
cally, but you, as a living person, cannot be known to me unless you reveal yourself. I can not discover you; unless you

take the initiative and reveal yourself, I cannot know you. The proof of the pudding here is the psychoanalytical couch. Suppose that I am sick. I go to a psychoanalyst. We get started after all the preliminaries are over, and what is the problem? The thing that is sick about me is my psyche. My doctor cannot take an x-ray of my psyche. So, what does he do if I am in bad shape? He gives me a drug to get me talking. Otherwise, he sets up a community of trust and encourages me to talk: 'Did you ever have any dreams? Tell me about the dreams. Just talk. What do you think the problem is?' What is the analyst doing? He is getting me to talk because he can not deal with my psyche diagnostically or therapeutically unless he can coach me into self-revelation.

The analyst cannot know me; I cannot know you; no person can be known unless that person comes out of hiding and reveals himself. We cannot know God unless God reveals himself. Christianity is inevitably and unchangeably grounded in God as God has revealed himself. The Bible is the record of that revelation, the revelation which came to living persons—to Amos or St. Paul, for example.

If we come, therefore, to teenagers with some understanding of their love-life, perhaps we can communicate to them the fact that at least one great historic view of life—one that has informed the whole history of our western culture and has spread throughout the world—says that life is broken, and twisted, and distorted unless we can learn to love God first and to love all God's creatures in the order of love which God has ordained. Here only is happiness.

There is self-fulfillment and true self-fulfillment in the love of self for God's sake. We can even say that about the Cross of Christ, 'Who for the joy that was set before him, endured the Cross despising the shame, and is set down at the right hand of the throne of God' (Hebrews 12:2). Self-fulfillment is even in the Cross because Christ loved himself for God's sake, and gave himself to God; he gave himself to God and

God raised him up to his own right hand.

Now, more profoundly, the teenager has a basic problem which everybody knows. It is the problem of authority. In asserting himself in the search for self-fulfillment, he resents not only authoritarianism or dictatorship, but also authority itself. Sin gives all human authority an authoritarian distortion, and all rebellion against authoritarianism is of an antinomian cast. The teenagers rebel not only against authoritarianism, but they rebel against authority itself. That is what makes their and our problem so hard. On the other hand, they cannot live without authority, and they know it acutely because they are not yet adults. They do not really believe they can live on their own, on their own authority. There is a wonderful story in the Episcopal Church's tenth grade teachers' manual. It is about a fifteen year old boy. When his father came home tired from a day's work, he noticed that the boy obviously had something important on his mind. Then the boy said, 'Dad, I would like to talk to you.' The father put his paper down. The boy continued, 'I've been thinking it over Dad, and I think I am old enough now to take over my own life, make all my decisions, when to get up, when to go to bed, whether to study or not to study. I wanted to talk this out with you and tell you that that is the way I feel about it. I think the time has come.' The father rose with a twinkle in his eye and said, 'This is the day I have been looking forward to since you were born. You cannot imagine with what joy I say yes to you. This is what it was all about—that you should some day come to this.' The boy said nothing and went off. About five minutes later he came back and said, 'Dad, I would like to talk to you again. Dad, what we said a minute ago, that does not mean that if I get in a jam you would not help me out, does it?' There you are. The declaration of freedom and independence which goes out into the world, a world that is suspended over a bottomless, frightening abyss; and the return to the security, the authority, and the orderly framework of the parent-child relationship.

Now, all adolescents are in oscillation between these two poles, and it always seems to me that just at the time that they are rebelling, we are asserting authority, and, perhaps, being authoritarian. And just at the time that they come back to us for a framework of discipline, we are being very permissive. This must be very confusing to them. Of course, this is just an exaggerated way of saying how difficult the whole relationship is. And I am presupposing what everybody knows, that it is a lot of fun.

On the continent and in Britain, there is still a predominant mood of rebellion against authority, and psychoanalysis is in support of this. Let us not be beguiled by this, however, into not recognizing that we have a different form of the same problem in America. We have rebellion against authority and authoritarianism, of course; but the deepest need of the American teenager—and this need will be in varying degrees according to their social background—the deepest need is for authority. They're hungry for authority. They are living in a world where meaninglessness has seeped up for years through the structure of its life. It is manifest on our stage; it is everywhere in our art. Existentialism is the catchword of the time. French existentialism says, 'Here I am a man, a funny kind of unique creature, a rational creature, a decisive creature. Now, out there, there are a lot of things—you, the world, the sun, the moon, human history. It is all ridiculous. There is no reason why it should be. Indeed, it is absurd. Look and see how absurd we all are. Everything is ridiculous and absurd. There is no meaning in anything. Everything floats on an abyss of nothingness.'

A friend of mine wrote about French existentialism. The title of the book is *Encounters With Nothingness*. What do I do then? Jean Paul Sartre says, 'What do you do? You create meaning heroically by your moment-to-moment decisions. We make meaning for life.' Now, nobody really can live this way. It is a kind of desperate stoic courage that accepts absolute defeat with as much grace as it can.

Why is it that Elvis Presley, with his cold-blooded and deliberate fusion of rhythm and hysteria, catches teenage life so strongly? Because, if meaninglessness is welling up through the fibre of the whole of human society, then one does not look to the past for any great meaning. St. Augustine, St. Bernard, those great councils of the Church that talk about Christology, they do not know anything about our situation. One uses one's ignorance and one's alienation from great literature as an excuse for saying that we are basically different from them. But if we are cut off from our past, we also see nothing in the future. It all goes into nothingness. So let us live in the sensate moment. You can do this by being right wing in politics, by getting a job with a big corporation where there is security, by living in a suburban home, and by being a member of a country club and going to its Saturday night dances. Or, you can live in the sensate moment by smoking marijuana, by belonging to the 'anti-virgin girls' clubs'; or, by listening to Elvis Presley.

Do you remember the motion picture of Aldous Huxley's *Brave New World* where they added a gadget by which one could *feel* what was going on on the screen? The movies become the feelies. A sensate world with no dependence on the past and with no expectation of anything in the future is a fortress against the meaninglessness, however poor it may be.

Have you ever looked in the faces of the juvenile criminals as they stare at us from our newspapers and magazines? They are innocent. They do not even know what they have done. The switch-blade artists, the 'Rebels without a Cause,' are not vicious so much as brazenly innocent, amoral.

Everywhere, in Presley music, in modern art, in our literature, man is confronted by this meaninglessness. Pathetic islands of sensateness are not strong enough to overcome it. The only power that can overcome the power of the abyss in you—and the power of the abyss is in you and your world, and slowly eroding you and your world away: you are going to die—the only power that can overcome the power of abyss in you and the power of abyss in our teenagers is the power of the almighty God, who created you and all that is out of nothing. He is the Light that overcometh all darkness. Against him no creaturely power and no nothingness can finally prevail.

SERVICE OF WORSHIP

Let us pray.

Almighty God, most blessed and most holy, before the brightness of whose presence the angels veil their faces; with lowly reverence and adoring love, we acknowledge thy infinite glory and worship thee, Father, Son, and Holy Spirit, eternal Trinity. Blessing and honor, and glory, and power be unto Thee, our God, forever and ever. *Amen.*

Almighty God, whose dwelling is with the humble and contrite heart; grant us thy mercy. For all that has been evil in our lives, for unholy thoughts and impure motives, for scorn of goodness, trifling with truth, and indifference to beauty, forgive us, O God. For any wrong we have done our fellow men, for loss of temper, for neglect of charity, for failure of justice, for whatever one may rightfully hold against us, forgive us, O God, for the sake of Jesus Christ, our Lord. *Amen.*

Eternal God, in whom is our health and our peace; how may we utter our need of thee? Our minds need thee to give them poise. Our wills need thee to give them strength. Our hearts need thee to give them quiet. We need thee as we labor for a better world. Very urgent is our need of thee, if we are to face persistent evil with hopeful determination. O thou, who understands us better than we understand ourselves, grant us a healing, heartening consciousness of thy presence, as revealed in Jesus Christ, our Lord. *Amen.*

Let us hear the word of God in the Gospel According to St. Luke, the fifth chapter, at the beginning.

'Now it came to pass while the multitude pressed upon him and heard the word of God, that he was standing by the lake of Gennesaret and he saw two boats standing by the lake: but the fishermen had gone out of them, and were washing their nets. And he entered into one of the boats, which was Simon's, and asked him to put out a little from the land. And he sat down and taught the multitudes out of the boat. And when he had left speaking, he said unto Simon, Put out into the deep, and let down your nets for a draught. And Simon answered and said, Master, we toiled all night and took nothing: but at thy word I will let down the nets. And when they had done this, they enclosed a great multitude of fishes; and their nets were breaking; and they beckoned unto their partners in the other boat, that they should come and help them. And they came and filled both the boats, so that they began to sink. But Simon Peter, when he saw it, fell down at Jesus' knees, saying, Depart from me; for I am a sinful man, O Lord. For he was amazed, and all that were with him, at the draught of the fishes which they had taken; and so were also James and John, sons of Zebedee, who were partners with Simon. And Jesus said unto Simon, Fear not; from henceforth thou shalt catch men. And when they had brought their boats to land, they left all, and followed him.'

May God bless unto us the reading of this holy word.

One of the facts that I keep warning my boys about at Duke in the preaching classes is that they must not preach allegorically. While it has a distinguished history in the Catholic Church, it has not seemed good, in recent years—it has not seemed honest—to preach allegorically.

Now, having said that, I want to look at this passage with you allegorically. The only defense I can offer is that many of the critics take it allegorically. This is a story of how Christianity left the Jews, at least it anticipates that Christianity would leave the Jews. It would go out into the world, cast its net and take a tremendous catch. Our Lord himself made more of it than just a miracle. He certainly used it as an analogy when he said to Simon, 'Fear not, henceforth thou shalt catch men'—not fish. As we return from this good conference, in which you have allowed me to share, I want just to say two things suggested by this passage, two things which may help you as you go to your prep schools, and help us who spoke to you as we go back to our seminaries. First, Jesus sent these fishermen, these disciples, back to where they had failed: 'We have toiled all night and caught nothing. Nevertheless, at thy word we shall let down the net.' He sent them back to where they had not been successful. There is a roughness to reality as Jesus faces it. Now, I know that some of you are going back to success—where you had been successful under God—and that is good. Some of you are going back to failure. Now, of course, you can do one thing with the failure. You can rationalize it and interpret it religiously, which is very dangerous. There is a story of a man who met a Carthusian monk and said, 'Sir, I know several of the orders in your church, but I do not know yours. What do you stand for?' The Carthusian who had a twinkle in his eye, said, 'We do not have the intellectual prowess of the Dominicans, and we do not have the liturgical flavor of the Benedictines; we are not distinguished for good works like the Franciscans, but, when it comes to humility, we are tops.' Now, there are some of us that say, 'Yes, we failed, and we failed under God:' and we are proud of our humility. Then we are humble because we are proud of our humility. Then we are proud again because we are humble. Just take failure in your stride. Get back into the same boat and take the same net. Go back. That is how life is.

That is the first thing I would say; and the second, and the only other thing I would say, is this: There was one difference from the previous night's fishing for these disciples. Jesus went with them. He sent Peter back, but he added his presence. Last night, as Dr. Hofmann was interpreting for us the last verses of Matthew, 'Lo, I am with you always,' my mind went back to one page from David Livingstone's journal. He tells how he was about to cross the border to another tribe, a tribe that had been hostile. He might well face death. He said that as he sat there, he flipped his Bible open and opened it to Matthew, the last chapter; and he read the verses, 'Go ye into all the world, and, lo, I am with you always.' He fastened on the words, 'Lo, I am with you always;' and then, in Victorian English, he wrote, ' "Lo, I am with you always." It is the word of a gentleman of the most strict and sacred honor. And that's an end of it. Tomorrow I shall cross the border.' Jesus went, too.

I think, perhaps, the most forgotten person of the Trinity is the Third, the Holy Spirit: the continuing activity of God, as understood in Christ, in the world today. And they caught men and women. The promise that was fulfilled.

Let us pray.

O Lord God, to whose blessed Son all men took their problems; create amongst us men and women trained to guide the choices and the lives of those about them. We know what perplexities and confusion surround us all, and beg thy forgiveness for what we have added to the frustration of friends and students. Make us affirmative to heal, sensitive to understand tragedy, skilled to recognize the sources of difficulty, humble enough to ask for help and constant in our hope for every child of Thy love. Grant that we may ever remember those committed to our care, not as cases but as persons, never using our knowledge as power, but with self-effacement and love; that our work may be done to thy glory and for the relief of men's estate; through Jesus Christ, our Lord. *Amen.*

Eternal God, who through thy spirit has bestowed excellent gifts upon thy seers, prophets, priests, and teachers; endue with thy grace for the teaching of thy gospel and the ministration of help to thy people, these, thy servants who now separate one from the other to return to their own schools. Sustain them in mind and body; nourish their spirits that they may nourish thy children. May their insight clarify their vision and their confidence in thee increase their faith. May their humility chasten their pride; their devotion challenge their strength; and their courage make them good soldiers of thy son. Through their ministry may whatsoever things are honorable, just, pure, and lovely, and of good report, be established in our schools. Grant them vision to know what thou wouldst have them do, and boldness to speak thy truth without fear of mortal man; and by thy guidance, and leadership, through them, may thy Son's Church rightly serve our generation; to our eternal good, and to the glory of thy Holy Name. *Amen.*

APPENDICES

I

THE COUNCIL FOR RELIGION IN INDEPENDENT SCHOOLS: An Historical Sketch

The present character and work of the Council for Religion in Independent Schools scarcely seems to be related to a series of student-led prayer meetings at Andover back in 1814. Yet the Council is in direct descent from such meetings as those held at Phillips Academy one hundred and forty years ago and from a Bible Society at Lawrenceville, started in 1822, as well as from the mid-nineteenth century Christian Fraternity at Exeter. Before the turn of this century, John R. Mott in his student work for the Y.M.C.A. was able to capitalize heavily on the traditions of such religious expression, and thus to develop the organization of similar groups in many other of the schools which he visited for such a purpose. It was under his inspiration that the first conference for preparatory school students only was held at Peddie in 1897.

After 1900, the Student Y.M.C.A. provided traveling secretaries to develop further this sort of 'volunteer' religious expression in the schools, one of whom—Boyd Edwards— later on became headmaster successively of The Hill School and Mercersburg Academy. Beginning in 1915 the Blairstown Preparatory School Conference became the focal point for this work and continued to be that for many years. Though the establishment of this Conference meant a physical break with the Northfield College Conference with which the preparatory school students had been meeting jointly for fourteen years, the Northfield traditions continued to characterize the meetings at Blairstown. By 1937, however, the development of student conferences at Northfield, Buck Hill Falls, Natural Bridge, and in the Chicago area, had so reduced the popularity of the Blairstown meeting that it was given up.

In October, 1932, the heads of many of the schools which had been sending students to these conferences met in Atlantic City. Boyd Edwards, then headmaster of Mercersburg, led the meeting and Harold Ingalls, now in charge of Y.M.C.A. work at the University of Illinois, acted as secretary. Heads of schools, including Frank Boyden, Samuel S. Drury, Richard Gummere, Endicott Peabody, Lewis Perry, Walter Haviland, Alfred Stearns, Horace Taft and J. Carter Walker were in attendance. They discussed among themselves the ways and means of strengthening the Faith among their students, and they listened to speeches delivered by Rufus Jones, Henry Van Dusen, Luther Weigle, and Francis Sayre. Out of this meeting came the impetus to lessen the old emphasis on volunteer student meetings and to strengthen the work of the student conferences. It was at this meeting and at subsequent ones that the Episcopal and the Quaker schools began to participate with greater vigor in the work of what by that time was called 'The National Preparatory School Committee of the Y.M.C.A.'

The movement grew and changed in emphasis to a point where leaders in the schools felt it should become independent. In 1950 the parent relationship was broken, and with the blessing of the Y.M.C.A., the Council for Religion in Independent Schools was born, though that name was not officially adopted unti 1952.

The Council, as presently constituted, is directed by a Board of Trustees, whose membership is drawn from leaders in the supporting schools; and its work is paid for out of annual gifts from the schools. In 1956-57, two hundred and forty-two schools, representing all parts of the country and all types of organization, contributed nearly ten thousand dollars, though nearly five hundred of our country's independent secondary schools are touched by the Council's work. Interested individuals and national church bodies have also made substantial contributions. The Danforth Foundation and the Hazen Foundation have recently assisted the Council generously in carrying out certain specified projects, such as the Yale Institute (a program for faculty-in-service training, designed primarily to clarify the Christian perspectives of the usual subjects in a school curriculum), and so-called Faculty Colloquia. The Colloquia are meetings of varying duration, conducted under expert guidance, for teachers of religion and other subjects, and for heads of schools in particular areas, at which problems of mutual interest are discussed. The student conferences at Buck Hill Falls, Northfield, Natural Bridge continue to be a great concern of the Council, as are newer ones at Cleveland and elsewhere. All of these conferences are now open to both boys and girls. A bulletin—*Religion in the Schools*—containing articles, occasional book reviews, and lists of recommended books, is published in mimeographed form several times a year. The work of the Council is carried out by a salaried Director and Executive Secretary, and by unpaid committees made up of heads or teachers in the schools. Recently, Regional Areas have been set up, each in charge of a chairman who is on the faculty of a school in that area. These chairmen work closely with the Director, especially in the planning of regional conferences or Faculty Colloquia.

The work of the Council nowadays bears very little outward resemblance to that voluntary expression of student piety so many generations ago at Phillips Academy at Andover. The piety remains, we hope, at the center of the Council's work—piety that is showing signs of a revived concern for sound theology and high scholarship.

II

DIRECTORY OF

CONFERENCE PARTICIPANTS

Adelphi Academy
Brooklyn, New York

Agnes Irwin School
Wynnewood, Pa.

Albany Academy
Albany, New York

Alexander Robertson School
New York, N. Y.

Allendale School
Rochester, N. Y.

Avon Old Farms School
Avon, Conn.

Baldwin School
Bryn Mawr, Pa.

Barnard School for Girls
New York, N. Y.

Baylor School
Chattanooga, Tenn.

Beard School
Orange, N. J.

Bishop's School
La Jolla, Calif.

Blair Academy
Blairstown, N. J.

Brearley School
New York, N. Y.

Brimmer and May School
Boston, Mass.

Brooklyn Friends School
Brooklyn, N. Y.

Brooks School
North Andover, Mass.

Brunswick School
Greenwich, Conn.

Bryn Mawr School
Baltimore, Md.

Cathedral School of St. Mary
Garden City, N. Y.

Charles E. Ellis School
Newton Square, Pa.

Chatham Hall
Chatham, Va.

Cheshire Academy
Cheshire, Conn.

Chestnut Hill Academy
Philadelphia, Pa.

Choate School
Wallingford, Conn.

Christchurch School
Christchurch, Va.

Collegiate School
New York, N. Y.

Cranbrook School
Bloomfield Hills, Mich.

Dana Hall School
Wellesley, Mass.

Darrow School
New Lebanon, N. Y.

Dwight School
Englewood, N. J.

Eaglebrook School
Deerfield. Mass.

Ellis School
Pittsburgh, Pa.

Emma Willard School
Troy, New York

Englewood School for Boys
Englewood, N. J.

Episcopal Academy
Philadelphia, Pa.

Episcopal High School
Alexandria, Va.

Ethel Walker School
Simsbury, Conn.

Fountain Valley School
Colorado Springs, Colo.

Foxcroft School
Middleburg, Va.

Friends Academy
Locust Valley, N. Y.

Friends' Central School
Philadelphia, Pa.

Friends School
Wilmington, Del.

Friends School
Baltimore, Md.

Friends School
Atlantic City, N. J.

Friends Select School
Philadelphia, Pa.

George School
George School, Pa.

Germantown Friends School
Philadelphia, Pa.

Gill School
Bernardsville, N. J.

Gilman School
Baltimore, Md.

Girard College
Philadelphia, Pa.

Greenhill School
Dallas, Texas

Greenwich Academy
Greenwich, Conn.

Greenwich Country Day School
Greenwich, Conn.

Grosse Pointe University School
Grosse Pointe, Mich.

Groton School
Groton, Mass.

Gunnery School
Washington, Conn.

Hackley School
Tarrytown, N. Y.

Miss Hall's School
Pittsfield, Mass.

Halsted School
Yonkers, N. Y.

Hamden Hall Country Day School
New Haven, Conn.

Hannah More Academv
Reisterstown, Md.

Hartridge School
Plainfield, N. J.

Haverford School
Haverford, Pa.

Hill School
Pottstown, Pa.

Hockaday School
Dallas, Texas

Holton-Arms School
Washington, D. C.

Horace Mann School
New York. N. Y.

Hotchkiss School
Lakeville, Conn.

House in The Pines
Norton, Mass.

Howe Military School
Howe, Indiana

Kent School
Englewood, Colo.

Kent Place School
Summit, N. J.

Kingswood School Cranbrook
Bloomfield Hills, Mich.

Lankenau School
Philadelphia, Pa.

Laurel School
Cleveland, Ohio

Lawrenceville School
Lawrenceville, N. J.

Lincoln School
Providence, R. I.

Longfellow School For Boys
Bethesda, Md.

Loomis School
Windsor, Conn.

Maret School
Washington, D. C.

Margaret Hall School
Versailles, Ky.

Masters School
Dobbs Ferry, N. Y.

Mercersburg Academy
Mercersburg, Pa.

Milton Hershey School
Hershey, Pa.

Milwaukee-Downer Seminary
Milwaukee, Wisc.

Montclair Academy
Montclair, N. J.

Moorestown Friends' School
Moorestown, N. J.

Moravian Seminary For Girls
Bethlehem, Pa.

Moses Brown School
Providence, R. I.

Mount Hermon School
Mount Hermon, Mass.

Mount Vernon Seminary
Washington, D. C.

National Cathedral School For Girls
Washington, D. C.

Newark Academy
Newark, N. J.

New Canaan Country School
New Canaan, Conn.

New York Military Academy
Cornwall, N. Y.

Nightingale-Bamford School
New York, N. Y.

Northampton School For Girls
Northampton, Mass.

Northfield School For Girls
East Northfield, Mass.

North Park Academy
Chicago, Ill.

Northwestern M. & N. Academy
Lake Geneva, Wisc.

Oakwood School
Poughkeepsie, N. Y.

Oxford School
Hartford, Conn.

Palmer Memorial Institute
Sedalia, N. C.

Peddie School
Hightstown, N. J.

Peekskill Military Academy
Peekskill, N. Y.

Pembroke-Country Day School
Kansas City, Mo.

Pennington School
Pennington, N. J.

Phillips Exeter Academy
Exeter, N. H.

Pingry School
Elizabeth, N. J.

Pomfret School
Pomfret, Conn.

Miss Porter's School
Farmington, Conn.

Prospect Hill School
New Haven, Conn.

Providence Country Day School
Providence, R. I.

Riverdale Country School
Riverdale, N. Y.

Rye Country Day School
Rye, New York

St. Agnes School
Albany, N. Y.

St. Agnes School
Alexandria, Va.

St. Alban's School
Washington, D. C.

St. Andrew's School
Middletown, Del.

St. Anne's School
Charlottesville, Va.

St. Bernard's School
New York, N. Y.

St. Catherine's School
Richmond, Va.

St. Christopher's School
Richmond, Va.

St. George's School
Newport, R. I.

St. Hilda's School
New York, N. Y.

St. Louis Country Day School
St. Louis, Mo.

St. Margaret's School
Waterbury, Conn.

St. Margaret's School
Tappahannock, Va.

St. Mark's School
Southborough, Mass.

St. Mark's School
Dallas, Texas

St. Mary's Hall
Faribault, Minn.

St. Mary's Hall
Burlington, N. J.

Saint Mary's-In-The-Mountains
Littleton, N. H.

St. Paul's School
Brooklandville, Md.

St. Paul's School
Concord, N. H.

St. Stephen's Episcopal School
Austin, Texas

St. Stephen's School
Alexandria, Va.

St. Thomas Church Choir School
New York, N. Y.

St. Timothy's School
Stevenson, Md.

Salisbury School
Salisbury, Conn.

Samuel Ready School
Baltimore, Md.

Scarborough Country Day School
Scarborough, N. Y.

Sewickley Academy
Sewickley, Pa.

Shady Side Academy
Pittsburgh, Pa.

Shattuck School
Faribault, Minn.

Shipley School
Bryn Mawr, Pa.

Southwest Episcopal School
Bellaire, Texas

Spence School
New York, N. Y.

Springside School
Philadelphia, Pa.

Stevens School
Philadelphia, Pa.

Stony Brook School
Stony Brook, N. Y.

Tatnall School
Wilmington, Del.

Texas Military Institute
San Antonio, Texas

Thayer Academy
So. Braintree, Mass.

Tower Hill School
Wilmington, Del.

Trinity School
New York, N. Y.

Upper Canada College
Ontario, Canada

Vail-Deane School
Elizabeth, N. J.

Valley Forge Military Academy
Wayne, Pa.

Western Reserve Academy
Hudson, Ohio

Westminster School
Simsbury, Conn.

Westover School
Middlebury, Conn.

Westtown School
Westtown, Pa.

William Penn Charter School
Philadelphia, Pa.

Winchester-Thurston School
Pittsburgh, Pa.

III

SUGGESTED READING

Theme: A PRACTICAL CHRISTIANITY

Baillie, John. *Invitation to Pilgrimage.*
New York: Charles Scribner's Sons, 1942.

Dodd, C. H. *The Bible Today.*
New York: Cambridge University Press, 1946.

Fosdick, H. E. *A Guide to Understanding the Bible.*
New York: Harper & Bros., 1938.

Lewis, C. S. *The Screwtape Letters.*
New York: Macmillan Co., 1943.

Murray, A. Victor. *Teaching the Bible.*
New York: Cambridge University Press, 1955.

Spurrier, Wm. A. *Guide to the Christian Faith.*
New York: Charles Scribner's Sons, 1952.

Wilder, Amos A. *Liberal Learning and Religion.*
New York: Harper & Bros., 1955.

Theme: CHRISTIAN REVELATION AND THE INSIGHTS
OF PSYCHOLOGY

Allport, G. W. *Becoming.*
New Haven: Yale University Press, 1955.

Horney, Karen. *Our Inner Conflicts.*
New York: W. W. Norton & Co., 1945.

Langer, Walter C. *Psychology and Human Living.*
New York: Appleton-Century-Crofts, 1943.

May, Rollo. *Man's Search for Himself.*
New York: W. W. Norton & Co., 1953.

Piaget, Jean. *The Child's Conception of the World.*
New York: Harcourt Brace & Co., 1929.

White, Robt. W. *Lives in Progress.*
New York: The Dryden Press, 1952.

Theme: THE MEANING OF LOVE IN CHRISTIAN THOUGHT

Bonthius, Robt. H. *Christian Paths to Self-Acceptance.*
    New York: King's Crown Press, 1955.

Casserley, J. V. L. *No Faith of My Own.*
    Greenwich: Seabury Press, 1950.

The Christian Scholar, Vol. XXXIX No. 1, March 1956,
    257 Fourth Ave., New York 10, N. Y.

Filson, Floyd V. *The New Testament Against Its Environment.*
    Chicago: Henry Regnery Co., 1950.

Herberg, Will. *Judaism and Modern Man.*
    New York: Farrar, Straus & Young, 1951.

Kunkel, Fritz. *In Search of Maturity.*
    New York: Charles Scribner's Sons, 1943.

Miller, Alexander. *The Renewal of Man.*
    New York: Doubleday & Co., 1955.

Outler, Albert. *Psychotherapy and the Christian Message.*
    New York: Harper & Bros., 1954.

Read, David H. C. *The Christian Faith.*
    New York: Charles Scribner's Sons, 1956.

Richardson, Alan. *The Gospel and Modern Thought.*
    New York: Oxford University Press, 1950.

Tillich, Paul. *The Courage to Be.*
    New Haven: Yale University Press, 1952.